Write a Bestselling Thriller

Matthew Branton

Matthew Branton is the author of novels including *The Love Parade, The House of Whacks, Coast* and *The Hired Gun*. In addition to working in publishing, and as a journalist and screenwriter, he has for many years provided editorial advice to first-time authors, helping them explore the key techniques of the craft of writing fiction and find satisfaction in their work.

Write a Bestselling Thriller

Matthew Branton

Hodder Education

338 Euston Road, London NW1 3BH.

Hodder Education is an Hachette UK company

First published in UK 2012 by Hodder Education

First published in US 2012 by The McGraw-Hill Companies, Inc

Copyright © 2012 Matthew Branton

The moral rights of the author have been asserted

Database right Hodder Education (makers)

The *Teach Yourself* name is a registered trademark of Hachette UK.

British Library Cataloguing in Publication Data: a catalogue record for this
title is available from the British Library.

Library of Congress Catalog Card Number: on file

10 9 8 7 6 5 4 3 2 1

The publisher has used its best endeavours to ensure that any website
addresses referred to in this book are correct and active at the time of going
to press. However, the publisher and the author have no responsibility for
the websites and can make no guarantee that a site will remain live or that
the content will remain relevant, decent or appropriate.

The publisher has made every effort to mark as such all words which it
believes to be trademarks. The publisher should also like to make it clear
that the presence of a word in the book, whether marked or unmarked, in
no way affects its legal status as a trademark.

Every reasonable effort has been made by the publisher to trace the
copyright holders of material in this book. Any errors or omissions should
be notified in writing to the publisher, who will endeavour to rectify the
situation for any reprints and future editions.

Hachette UK's policy is to use papers that are natural, renewable and
recyclable products and made from wood grown in sustainable forests.
The logging and manufacturing processes are expected to conform to the
environmental regulations of the country of origin.

www.hoddereducation.co.uk

Cover image © mipan – Fotolia

Typeset by Cenveo Publisher Services.

Printed in Great Britain by CPI Group (UK) Ltd, Croydon, CR0 4YY.

**Also available
in ebook**

Contents

Design and publicity
Publication – reviews, interviews and public events
What next?
Other publishing alternatives

Introduction

For a thriller writer, this book is a labour of love. I've been lucky enough to publish several thrillers internationally, which has opened many interesting doors over the years.

One of the most rewarding has been to work with new novelists, writer to writer. I've read hundreds of debut novels, written by people from all walks of life, and compiled detailed editorial analyses of each. My clients' subsequent successes have shown me how ideas about storytelling can be passed from writer to writer: insights about the nuts and bolts of the craft, techniques to prime the cogs and flywheels and pistons of the thriller engine.

It's also been my luck to have the chance to talk fiction with many other writers, in my career as a novelist. But before that, I had the good fortune to see things from the industry side of the storytelling business.

After graduation, I laboured up the publishing ladder to a job at a big fiction house: a place where I could put questions to people who knew. I asked the most pressing, for me at least: what does it take to make a living from writing fiction?

The answer I heard, from booksellers to bestselling novelists, was this: write stories that reward readers.

I thought about the novels that had rewarded me most often over the years, and wrote a thriller. It went down well, so I wrote a few more. In time I got to talk shop with the writers and directors who'd influenced me, and take what I learned from them into my own writing. But I've also put it into my work with budding novelists, exploring ideas about plot, character, dramatic structure, and bringing it all together on the page.

This book is the fruit of the many insights about storytelling I've been lucky enough to hear, from novelists and agents, from publishers and big-volume booksellers. I am similarly indebted to the great thriller authors of our time, whose works and professional insights give invaluable example to students of storytelling. But ultimately I'm indebted, like thriller authors everywhere, to the readers whose enthusiasm and thirst for adventure make this high-octane genre an exciting place to work.

Matthew Branton

Acknowledgements

Quotation from Frederick Forsyth CBE (Chapter 1), from an interview originally broadcast by the RNIB's Insight Radio, reproduced with kind permission of Frederick Forsyth and of Robert Kirkwood of Insight Radio.

Thrillers: What They Are and What They Do

In this chapter you will learn:

- ► *What a thriller is, exactly*
- ► *Why thrillers can offer you unparalleled opportunities to win a wide readership*
- ► *The essential difference between crime fiction, or mystery novels, and thrillers*
- ► *What thrillers deliver on the page*

Why write thrillers?

'I had probably the best motivation there ever was. I was skint.'

Frederick Forsyth

As you might expect from a master storyteller, there's both a plain truth and a world of subtext in that wry quote.

Frederick Forsyth is one of the greatest thriller authors of all time. His novels are famed for both their colossal sales and edge-of-seat movie adaptations: *The Day of the Jackal, The Odessa File, The Dogs of War*. Forsyth sat down to write his first masterpiece after a brilliant early career.

Starting as the youngest pilot to serve his country's Air Force, Forsyth spread his wings to become an international reporter, ultimately covering Africa's fiercest warzones.

There, in the depths of hell, Forsyth faced a formidable dilemma. He solved it by publishing an incisive analysis of the conflict, then deciding what to do with the rest of his life. Luckily, for millions of avid readers and film-fans, he chose to write thrillers.

Another colossus of the thriller world has an even more intriguing backstory. Destined to become one of the most acclaimed authors of our era, his career began in a rather more perilous sphere – he was recruited by British Intelligence while still in his teens.

A high-level career followed. It's said to have been ended, along with many others, by one of the most notorious 'double-agent' betrayals ever. But the young intelligence officer, with big achievements already beneath his belt, had another.

Writing under the pen-name John le Carré, he was also a bestselling novelist. Twenty-some thrillers later, he is hailed internationally as a literary genius and master storyteller.

Lee Child, one of the most successful thriller authors of our time, is yet another big achiever. A law-school graduate, he took up a career in television, working on a stupendous amount of broadcasting at one of the biggest studios in the business.

Been there, done that. Lee Child then famously splashed out the sum of six dollars on pencils and paper and sat down to become, in his own words, 'an American thriller writer'. More than a dozen international bestsellers down the line, his place in publishing history is assured.

The top of the game

Some of the biggest names in thrillers are certainly high-flyers: lawyers who have won millions of readers with courtroom thrillers, pathologists who have become publishing phenomena with forensic thrillers. Serious professionals, people who've excelled in highly-specialized fields, seem almost invariably – when the time comes to pursue their literary dreams – to choose thrillers.

And some start out that way. The biggest names in storytelling of our times – Spielberg, Scorsese, the Coen brothers, the late Michael Crichton (of *Jurassic Park* and *ER* fame) – cut their teeth on thrillers, and return again and again to them through their careers.

The most memorable movie characters of the last few decades – the ones whom people all over the world quote to each other, and are always instantly recognized – were conceived and made famous by thriller novelists (consider a certain Brit who prefers his Martinis shaken, not stirred, and a clever chap fond of fava beans and fine Chianti). Wherever there are all-time best-loved book lists, and all-time box-office smashes, there are thrillers.

So what is it about thrillers that makes them the most-quoted, most talked-about stories on the planet? What is it about thrillers that attracts achievers to write them?

In this exploration of the craft of the thriller, we'll take lessons from some of the biggest names in the game:

- **Thomas Harris,** author of the Hannibal Lecter thrillers

- **John le Carré,** author of the *Tinker Tailor Soldier Spy* trilogy (memorably filmed with Alec Guinness, and more recently Gary Oldman, as spymaster George Smiley)

- **Elmore Leonard,** whose streetwise thrillers delight literati and box-office alike: the *Get Shorty* series, Tarantino's *Jackie Brown*, Soderbergh's *Out of Sight*

- **Lee Child,** author of the globally bestselling Jack Reacher series

- **Ian Fleming,** creator of the most enduring thriller hero of all time: James Bond

All of these market-makers use the core principles of thriller writing again and again in their work:

- *characterization* developed with *deep character*

- at-stake *plotting* with vigorous *escalation*

- 'hookline' story *triggers*

- end-of-the-line *conflicts*

- three-act *dramatic structure*

- escalating mid-act and act *climaxes*

- powerful plot twists, or *reversals*

- full-resolution *showdowns*

We'll study these techniques and principles in detail. But let's begin with one of the most rewarding aspects of the thriller genre, for any writer or student of life.

The scope of thrillers

If you're fascinated by life – in all its wonder and detail and diversity – and you want to write about it, then the thriller genre may be the best game in town.

Let's look at the alternatives. 'Literary fiction' tends to focus on tiny slices of life. Its delicately nuanced stories call for sharp focus: metaphorically broad, perhaps, but in practical on-the-page terms, zoomed sharply in to catch nuance.

Which narrows the perimeter. Jane Austen spoke of the literary-fiction canvas as a 'little bit of ivory (two inches wide) on which I work with so fine a brush'. If what fascinates you is the breadth and depth of human experience, you may want more than a couple of inches to work on.

'Romance' fiction is a genre closer in some respects to the thriller, in that plot and character carry more weight, but it still operates within a clearly defined and closed world. Opposites may attract, and principal characters may come from dizzyingly different spheres, but the space the couple create between them is the world of the love story. Again, Austen and her two inches of ivory.

Historical fiction ties its narrative to the fine detail of a particular time and place. Whodunnits are similarly limited to the minutiae of the situation in hand. But in thrillers, the only limits are those of your imagination, savvy and ingenuity.

Remember this

In thriller fiction, the world is truly your oyster. And – very unlike Tinseltown or TV – your locations, stars and stunts come free.

In the opening scene of a thriller, the story might hang on haggling etiquette amongst Himalayan horse-traders. The next scene could follow a billionaire on to a Monte Carlo mega-yacht. The very next could be in a Chiang Mai opium den.

Each of these worlds will be evoked with equal depth, detail and fidelity by the thriller author. Each will have been as meticulously researched, imagined and fleshed-out in the story. And the very next scene may take the reader somewhere else entirely, as the free-ranging scope of the thriller draws yet more of life, and of human experience, into its viewfinder.

Why readers love thrillers

But is that all there is to the appeal of thrillers? Their wide-ranging panorama?

Thrillers are sometimes dismissed as 'airport fiction'. There's truth in that: airport bookstores sell a lot of thrillers. But it's easy to misread what this means.

Who are the people with planes to catch? Many are people on work trips. If they're flying from place to place to do their business, they're good at what they do, and no doubt busy too. But, to provide for the precious moments of free time they can snatch on the road, they go to the airport bookstore.

Browsing the shelves next to them might be the next most frequent-flyers: folk heading off on holiday. These are people who are living the most dreamed-about moment of their entire year: the morning when, instead of hurrying to work, they pack a bag with their favourite clothes and set off to focus entirely on pleasure and recreation for a little while. They work all year for this moment and now it's here. The airport bookstore knows what these people want too.

Who else catches planes? People on family visits: for weddings, births, anniversaries. People responding to crises: accidents, deaths, sudden illnesses of loved ones. People, in short, who are heading off to have powerful emotional experiences, possibly the most profound of their lives. What do they take along, to fortify and sustain them? A glance around any airport bookstore will show you.

Try it now

Bookstores are great places to get a feel for the many different types of thriller, to see for yourself what they can offer you as a writer. So take a notepad to the thriller section of a bookstore, or find a specialist thriller bookstore online, and browse the titles as if you've set out to find a good read today. Which novels grab you the most at first sight, without reading the 'blurbs'? What do the titles and cover designs of these books say to you? Write down the things that really stand out to you.

There's an old adage that you should write what you love, and there's a lot of truth in it – if you're to write in your chosen genre for long enough to build a career in it, then your chosen genre must be one you can realistically see yourself still getting fired-up about when you're many novels down the line.

So take a new sheet of paper and write down the qualities you associate with the kind of thrillers you want to write.

✱ If you pick up on things like a tough hero, an urgent situation and a fast-paced chase, then *action thrillers* are probably your kind of story.

✱ If society's true power-plays are what intrigue you, then there are a range of thriller genres for you to choose from:

▷ *Political thrillers* are about what really goes down at the top table.

▷ *Business thrillers* focus on corruption and fraud, often inspired by real-world excesses.

▷ *Historical thrillers* often focus on the prime movers of an era at a critical moment in their machinations, often in order to comment on present-day abuses.

✱ If a good old-fashioned life-or-death hunt with everything on the line is what floats your boat then *cop thrillers*, *spy thrillers* and *combat thrillers* all have a lot to offer.

✱ If pushing the limits of horror and dramatic possibility are what keeps you turning pages, then *supernatural thrillers* may be fertile ground for you.

So how do your two sheets of paper match up? Is the kind of thriller you want to write the kind of thriller you want to read? For a detailed explanation of thriller genres, with suggestions for key novels to inspire you on your journey as a thriller aficionado, turn to the Glossary at the back of this book.

Facing down the dragon: thrillers and mythology

One of the most brilliant exchanges of dialogue ever written comes with the hero in desperate straits. The kind that makes you squirm, a whole half-century after thriller-supremo Ian Fleming created it. In this famous showdown, the hero is strapped – wrists and ankles – to a steel table. A laser beam is advancing rapidly between his forcibly spread legs. The laser is cutting through the thick steel of the table like a blowtorch through butter. In a very few seconds, it will cut the hero in half: groin first.

Bond: Do you expect me to talk?

Goldfinger: No, Mr Bond. I expect you to die.

Thrillers deal with the big situations in life. They deal with the big questions. Sometimes in small ways; sometimes in the most pyrotechnic – or otherwise painful – way possible.

Thrillers take on the toughest question, in life's incessant struggle between Might and Right. It's the question which drives religions, philosophies, and political ideologies; the conundrum mankind has grappled with more than any other. It's more complex than the currency markets, more thorny than a thicket of briar strung with barbed wire, and goes all the way back to a certain apple tree with a snake twined round its trunk. The question is this:

We have free will – how should we use it?

In Celtic mythology, in tales told by firelight in the depths of harsh northern winters, one figure recurs: a lone warrior, backed into a corner deep underground, faced by a dragon. It's not possible for the warrior to win – this is an actual hellfire dragon, when fairytales of St George were yet to be written. So the outcome is not the point of the story; the warrior will die. What matters is how valiantly he fights.

What thrillers deliver

This is the heart of the thriller. A heroine might be a resourceful, highly skilled soldier, with the tools and talent to face down anything the world can throw at her. Or the hero might be a little guy, a nine-to-fiver sucked into a conspiracy when all he craves is a quiet life. Both will be tested to their limits and beyond by the skilled thriller writer, pitting the devil's own against a lone, cornered mortal.

Thriller plots can play out anywhere in the world, in any sphere of human existence or endeavour. Thriller characters can come from any walk of life. But what all thrillers have in common is that they interrogate the toughest question. Do we lie down before the dragon? Do we try, desperately, to bargain? Or do we stand and fight?

Key idea

Thrillers are stories about how people stand their ground when the chips are truly down. They tell human stories of self-sufficiency, courage and survival.

We owe our existence to our ancestors. For most of human history, life was harsh and cruel. Yet our forebears fought to survive despite the odds stacked against them.

Thrillers speak to this indomitable human spirit, which is why readers respond to them so consistently. They deliver a powerful emotional experience that confirms our humanity.

Of course, thrillers often achieve this in the most double-edged, bittersour and backhanded of ways, but such is life. Thrillers are never naively moralistic, and rarely does good trump evil entirely.

Instead, thrillers are modern-day parables of how good and evil co-exist in the world. And how good can have the upper hand, if – and only if – we keep human values alive.

Key idea

Readers respond to stories which tackle the questions they face in their own lives. For centuries, storytellers have taken these questions and put them into intensified projections of life's struggles: 'plots'.

Practical exercise: what is a thriller?

The fuel of a thriller is mystery. A puzzle must be solved, or a predicament escaped. Usually these feature a crime, or several. But many crime novels aren't thrillers, and some thrillers don't feature crimes at all. So what defines a thriller?

The answer is simple. A thriller is a mystery which pushes jeopardy to the end of the line.

Here's what it looks like in practice. Consider the following plot outline:

A body is found. It looks like a natural death, but a tenacious cop proves it was murder. As soon as the murder is made public, cryptic messages begin to arrive from someone claiming to be the killer, taunting the police. Another body is found; back at base another note arrives. Then another body, another note.

The cop goes through each victim's life with a fine-tooth comb, and finds several reasons why someone could have wanted each person dead. They turn out to be blind alleys. She tries to find a connection between the victims but there is none.

The cryptic messages step up, mocking the cop. But reverse engineering the blind alleys leads her to someone who 'can't' have committed crimes, who 'can't' be sending the messages, yet had means and motive for one of the murders. She thinks the unthinkable – two people have been murdered simply to muddy her investigation of a third. She sets an ingenious trap and catches the killer.

This is not a thriller. It's strewn with dead bodies from the start, it has an investigation full of twists, a heroic battle of wits, and opportunities for suspense by the bucketload, but it's not a thriller – it's a mystery, a crime novel.

Now look at this plot outline:

A body is found. It looks like a natural death, but a tenacious cop proves it was murder. As soon as the murder is made public, cryptic messages begin to arrive from someone claiming to be the killer, taunting the police. Another body is found, still warm, with one of these cryptic notes stuffed into its mouth.

The cop goes through both victims' lives with a fine-tooth comb, and finds several reasons why someone could have wanted each person dead. They turn out to be blind alleys. She tries to find a connection between the victims but there is none.

The cryptic messages step up, mocking the cop. Then she finds one, at home, pinned to her pillow. It says she's out of time. A clue in the note leads her to a third body – her assistant. No note on the body this time.

The cop sets an ingenious trap, with herself as bait. No one shows, but her phone rings. It's her boss: she's off the case, suspended from work, while her assistant's line-of-duty death is investigated. A police car rolls up, and she's stripped of her badge and her gun. She smashes her phone in frustration, goes to a bar, gets drunk and staggers home. Messages wait on her answerphone – all from her ex who is frantic. Their daughter has disappeared from kindergarten: vanished into thin air. A cryptic note was found taped to the school railings. Six hours ago, while the cop was downing her first shot of rye.

This is a thriller. It cranks up what's at stake in the story, and keeps cranking it. There are the same number of corpses as the mystery story, but a whole world more *jeopardy*. That jeopardy starts with the cop's reputation and professional standing. Then it escalates to mortal jeopardy: people are getting killed while the cop flounders.

In the second plot outline, above, the jeopardy zeroes-in on the cop's own mortality – the death-threat pinned to her pillow. It follows through with the body of her close colleague.

We don't think it can get any worse, but the story pushes it to the end of the line: the mortal jeopardy of her only child. This ghastly bad day has escalated from professional and personal jeopardy to catastrophic jeopardy of the core self.

Jeopardy kicks in, with both stories, at the start. It escalates in both until the cop's whole career is at stake, even her self-belief.

A mystery writer will focus in on this particular aspect. The cop will have pressing personal demons to fight down as she pursues the killer. A skilled storyteller will make the twists and turns of her quest resonate deeply. We'll finish such a mystery novel satisfied and rewarded by the ingenuity and insight of both heroine and author.

But in the thriller plot, outlined in the second example above, the cop is in hell. Everything that happens is the very worst thing that can possibly go down at that point. The cop's self-belief is sorely tested? Then let's kill her assistant, and fill her with mortal guilt too. Couldn't feel more under fire? Let's take away her gun and her badge. Alone and helpless? Then let's give the killer her beloved only child, plus a six-hour head start.

In mystery fiction the author engages the reader with ingenuity. We're a problem-solving species, and the mystery writer makes an intriguing wager with the reader: *bet you can't solve this before I do.*

In thrillers, we engage both the head and the guts. We push jeopardy to the end of the line. We throw the protagonist into the flames, then commence hosing on kerosene.

In some thrillers, the flames are white-collar crimes, and the kerosene is corruption. Sometimes the flames are actual flames, and the kerosene is napalm.

What all thrillers do is create a dragon, and a cornered warrior. The question is not if the warrior will win – winning looks quite impossible – but how valiant the fight.

Why thrillers are thrilling

I've chewed the fat with many thriller novelists in my time, and a few thriller film-makers too, so I've heard a lot of reasons why people get into the game. They range from a childhood love of big thumping stories, to a professional desire to push writing skills as far as they can go.

But what I never hear is someone who just one day got the best idea ever: they came up with a 'knock 'em dead' plot twist that no one else had ever thought of – or a serial killer so extreme the story wrote itself.

Thrillers are about escalating stories. They put something at stake, and then they raise the stakes. All successful thrillers begin with something at stake in the story; it can be something as simple as whether or not the heroine gets her job done in the next hour or not.

A thriller's job from that point forward is to escalate what's at stake. Crank it up until the heroine's whole world – past, present and future – is on the line. Stage a scorching showdown, type 'The End', and you're done.

That doesn't sound like much, but I've just described one of the most successful thriller novels – and one of the most quoted movies – of all time. Its villain's name is as well-known worldwide as that of a certain fizzy brown beverage. The story is celebrated for its fiendish twists, its riveting dialogue and the gut-churning tension of its scenes, but its writer started out with none of those – just a heroine whom he planned to push to the end of the line.

The story is *The Silence of the Lambs* and its author is Thomas Harris. In his novel, Harris showcased the most memorable villain since the James Bond books, and some of the most edge-of-seat scenes in the history of storytelling. He brought his readers to unprecedented heights of tension, and matched those heights with extremes of horror.

But the seed of his story wasn't a cultured, brilliant man who happens to be a cannibal; nor was it that horrible gobbling noise Lecter makes in the movie. Harris' blistering story begins with a rookie cop who thinks the world is black and white: good guys on one side, bad guys on the other. How, the master storyteller mused, do I take this particular rookie to the end of the line?

Try it now

Building a blaze, then pitching kerosene on the flames in order to create and develop compelling action, is the thriller author's core skill set. Putting a protagonist in jeopardy, then pushing that jeopardy to the end of the line is the basic template for thriller story design. Consider the following scenarios:

✱ A cop must hunt a serial killer amongst the backwoods compounds of US fundamentalist militias.

✱ In a volatile third-world country, an NGO water-engineer sees evidence that a brutal warlord's outrages are funded by Western missionaries.

✱ The daughter of a Chinese general – and CIA asset – is abducted by Tibet protestors.

Give yourself ten minutes of blue-sky thinking with each, and jot down as many ideas as you can. Think of ways to intensify each plot, to add fuel to the flames. When you're done, take a fresh sheet of paper for each scenario and review your notes. Transfer the ideas that grab you most to your fresh sheet, and see if you can begin to sketch connections between

Progressing and developing plots in this structured way is much of the art of thriller writing. As with all difficult tasks, preparation is key to designing plot progressions, so give yourself plenty of time to begin working with these skills now – we'll explore their depth and utility throughout the journey of writing a novel, from story-design to final draft, in the chapters to come.

Who should read this book?

If you've invented the most horrible serial killer ever, then read on. If you think you've come up with the most fiendish final-scene reversal in the history of plot twists, and just need a story to get to this final scene, this book will help you too. If you think your hero's got legs because he or she owns a vineyard, sculpts masterpieces and whips up a mean *tagine* in the obligatory state-of-the-art kitchen, read on too. A good story will be needed to float all that, and we're going to look in detail at the craft of storytelling.

If you've come to this book with nothing but interest in thrillers, and the hunger to write them, then this book is your guide and reference manual. With illuminating examples from bestsellers and market makers, insights into what makes thrillers tick, and practical exercises to develop your skills, we'll explore in depth the tools of compelling storytelling:

▶ designing what's *at stake* in the story

▶ fleshing out *characterization* with *deep character*

▶ escalating *plot*

▶ turbo-charging plot escalation with rollercoaster *character arcs*

▶ nailing satisfying *resolutions* for both plots and characters

Thrillers need strong stories by definition. They're not just about splashing more gore around than the last guy, or making the killer a Beethoven buff who turns his victims into piano strings, or making the hero do all of his incisive thinking when, and only when, he's savouring a Cuban cigar over a chess game.

Thrillers are about taking something very basic – something very human – and pushing it to the end of the line.

Remember this

Exotic villains and super-tough heroes have always made for thrilling stories. But some of the biggest-selling thrillers of all time have ordinary, flawed people as heroes and villains. What matters in a thriller isn't the body count or the bullets and bombs, but facing down and surviving till 'the end of the line'.

Thriller writers use the tools of storytelling to take stories to the end of the line, and keep the action coming right up to the last page. In the chapters to come, we'll explore every trick of the trade which thriller authors use to achieve their page-turning effects. We'll start in the next chapter by focusing in on the key components of all thrillers – those high-octane ideas and knockout twists, and how authors train their minds to think them up. First, let's recap the key ideas for you to take forward.

The Thriller Author's Toolbox

In this chapter you will learn:

- ► *How thriller novelists get great ideas*
- ► *How authors train their brains to generate plot twists, suspense and big surprises*
- ► *How to use your day job, whatever it is, to help you develop as a budding author*
- ► *How to find space and time to write*

Ideas: inspiration versus perspiration

So what do you need to write a thriller? Let's take a detailed look at what a novelist needs to set out on the job.

For most budding writers, top of the list of essentials is this:

AN IDEA

An Idea with a capital I. The killer concept that can clinch a deal for a novel before a word is written. A big-calibre idea which sells a story on the title and tagline alone.

In Hollywood this is called *high-concept*. The kind of story that's so strong, it can be told in 25 words or less.

To illustrate, a thriller classic. In Elmore Leonard's *Out Of Sight*, a cop begins a passionate affair with a robber – while she's hunting him.

Thirteen words there – barely half the number mandated in Tinseltown for the very tightest stories. The latter tend to keep hero and villain strongly engaged, so in *Out Of Sight* Leonard pushed the concept as far as it can go. The cop and robber are so locked in combat that they're meeting in hotels to engage in battle on every human level possible. High-concept indeed, and brilliantly filmed with George Clooney and Jennifer Lopez, but an idea generated simply by taking a basic conflict – cop and robber – and pushing it to a logical extreme.

Try it now

What's your thriller genre of choice? Spy, action, cop, historical, political or business thrillers? Choose one, then think of the baddest possible bad-ass in your chosen world. What attributes make them so? What kind of training produced these attributes? What's their day job now? What kind of personality makes for this kind of bad-ass? What kind of background and personal history? How would this character come across, if you met them at a beach resort, found yourselves the only English-speakers in a far-flung bar late at night? Now the big question: is this a hero or a villain?

In this chapter we'll study ideas, discovering how writers train their brains to generate them. We'll look in detail at those all-important sparks of inspiration, using in-depth case studies to examine how classic thrillers were conceived, and developed from idea stage.

We'll move on to the dynamic components that all thrillers need, exploring how each is conceived and put to use. Character and conflict, twists and triggers, heroes and villains; we'll even cover that perennial problem for budding writers – finding time and space to develop, when you're busy making a living.

But let's begin with the beginning of all novels: the idea. How can we trigger those precious sparks of inspiration?

Try it now

Pick out the thrillers that have grabbed you most over the years. Jot down a few things you liked most about each – how the conflict of the novel was delivered, for example, or the way the hero develops, or the ingenuity of the plot, or the great twist at the end. Now flip through the novels and re-read those moments – examine how they're delivered on the page.

Perhaps there's a lot of well-used technical detail in those all-out chases, to make them convincing and keep escalating the action – *research* would be the skill at heart here. If the character of the hero is what grabbed you about a certain thriller, write down a few ways in which you can see that character being delivered on the page – the contrast between how they are 'on the job' and how they are in person might be one of them. In this example, *character development* could summarize the key skill. Soon you'll see for yourself that once you start breaking down ideas, the skills and thought processes used to construct them on the page begin to stand out. It's these skill sets – and the brain-training that generates them – which we'll explore in detail through the coming chapters, until you're ready to try a guided exercise in full-on thriller construction for yourself.

Working the day job: thinking like a novelist

At the start of this book we looked at the backstories of a few of the thriller greats, the routes they took to begin their writing careers. One thing they had in common was life experience, in spades. Forsyth, le Carré, Lee Child: they'd all done a lot with their lives before they started spinning yarns.

Well shoot, you might be justified in thinking. The route to writing novels for most of us is not to have a glittering career first, but to spend years working mind-numbing jobs in order to fund writing time. Novels take a long time to write, and you don't get paid till after you finish. So, like many other budding novelists, as a youth I earned money any way I could, to pay for a precious few weeks each year when I did nothing but write.

So for years I tended bars, worked nightshifts maintaining big-box computers, treated beachgoers for sunstroke and stings, hustled as a freelance journalist. I wouldn't describe any of these positions as particularly illuminating, but they weren't just lost time. In each job I had co-workers, people just as bum-achingly bored as I was, and ready to talk about all kinds of things in their lives if it meant passing the time. Even the most vapid, dead-end job can yield life experience by the bucketload if you go looking for it.

Remember this

If it feels like your nine-to-five is suffocating your creativity, then chat to your colleagues more. When you finally make it as a published author, and spend most of your time alone in a quiet room, you won't want to look back and regret not having made the most of your opportunities to talk to regular, working joes – at a time when they were your peers and workmates, not your market.

Brain-training: read before writing

All novelists have day jobs when they start out. Novels take a long time to write, and everyone's got to make a living meanwhile.

Some novelists are lucky enough to find rewarding careers to pay the bills along the way, but something everyone does on their journey to becoming a writer – really putting in the hours on this one – is read.

Published books are written to be read and enjoyed. If you enjoy fiction, you can pick up ideas about characterization, conflict, plot twists – all the essentials of storycraft. If you read books specifically about thriller components – non-fiction works on crime, combat, policing and intelligence – then you'll be adding to your professional knowledge. Even if you read nothing but nature books and *National Geographic*, you'll have a trove of interesting scene-setting and location-building detail.

So read everything and anything you're inclined to. The very process of seeking out facts and soaking them up exercises your mental faculties. It trains you to categorize, make connections, deduce, develop insights. Have you heard that we use only a tiny fraction of our brains' processing power? Reading to broaden your horizons is like giving your brain a hardware and operating-system upgrade.

Research in the online era

A novelist whose first big deal was literally front-page news mused to me on the pitfalls of research soon afterwards. She said the trouble with it was you could wind up justifying anything in the interests of research. Living in your jim-jams, getting everything delivered? You're researching social isolation. Waking up six days a week with your head in the toilet? You're researching wine.

She was joking, but she had a point. Time was, if you wanted to find out about a human activity, either you did it for yourself, or you paid an arm and a leg for the sole book on the subject.

Now, of course, things are very different. Google and Wikipedia and suchlike have changed, forever, the way writers research. When you need to know something for certain, the facts are only a couple of clicks away.

Or are they? I'm not so sure. A recent high-profile scandal in the UK showed that even Wikipedia is vulnerable to long-term malicious interference. Wikipedia has teams of administrators and fact-checkers dedicated to making their site an authoritative resource, yet it seems the system is still vulnerable. And very few other reference sites have an editorial set-up. It's wise therefore, I reckon, to take what you read online with an occasional barrowful of rock salt.

As for the almighty search engines, it's worth remembering that they only index the most-used parts of the internet. The rest of what's out there, you're on your own. A big sell of the internet for many people is it means that anyone can share their knowledge. But for the majority of the web, if you don't know the exact address – down to the last slash and squiggle – it might take a while for you to find it.

The internet is useful for many things but instant access to solid facts is not chief among them. However, it's still excellent at its original purpose – to bring people together, cheaply and easily. If you need to talk to an expert on a particular subject, it takes a matter of seconds to find them and bang off an email. If they don't mind sharing their knowledge, and most true experts like nothing more, you can Skype face-to-face at your convenience.

But chances are that an expert will have put what you need to know in a book. Developing a hunger for expert views in print is something anyone can do. So let's look at how reading anything and everything can help a thriller author in practice.

Getting ideas: behind the headlines

In Michael Tolkin's literary noir thriller *The Player*, a boardroom of Hollywood execs joke about dispensing with screenwriters entirely. Writers are expensive; they're also temperamental, self-absorbed, and have a conception of time which makes the Spanish *mañana* seem urgent. So the Hollywood execs pass the morning newspaper around, picking stories out at random, working each headline into a power-pitch idea for a blockbusting movie.

They seem to do pretty well, and smugly congratulate each other. But mostly what they're talking about is marketing and demographics, not stories. They're ideas designed to produce movie-poster hooklines for standard Hollywood claptrap. The scene is a nice little satire within the larger, savage satire of an incisive thriller.

So can thrillers be written from news stories? Thrillers are about crimes and conspiracies; the daily news is full of the very latest crimes and conspiracies. It seems a simple enough equation, so many budding thriller authors begin by taking an idea from a news story, and trying to work it up into a full-length thriller.

But most find that it's like trying to build a bookcase by gathering fallen branches and hammering them together, instead of using planks. The fallen branches are made of wood, the substance required for a bookcase; but planks are designed and shaped for the job in hand, are much easier to work with, and produce a far better end result.

Key idea

News stories can yield insights into how criminals operate, but successful thrillers don't just import real-life events and fictionalize them. As we'll explore in the chapters to come, the process of generating compelling characters and involving action is more structured and thoughtful than simply 'borrowing' wholesale from a news story.

Case study: turning research into compelling action

Lee Child is the undisputed king of research. Each of his mega-selling 'Jack Reacher' novels contains dozens of fascinating facts, all memorable, all brilliantly used, and many debunking thriller clichés.

In one of his early novels, for example, the hero has to hit another guy and put him on the floor. But instead of just having Reacher take a swing and be done with it, Child explores his hero's options.

First off, he decides to wallop his adversary on the side of the head, not in the mouth. Common sense says that a punch landed squarely on the face is going to hurt more than one on the ear, but Reacher – a former military cop, veteran of hundreds of barrack-room brawls – knows better.

And he's right. Think about it. Through the entirety of human evolution we had no effective lighting; our ancestors must have been constantly walking into walls in the dark. As a consequence, we can take a blow to the front of the head pretty well and, though our noses might bleed and we may have to spit out a few teeth, we pretty much keep on ticking. Hence the sport of boxing.

However, very few people in human history have managed to walk into a wall sideways. It's hard to do. Consequently, a blow to the side of the head is massively disorienting. Take a solid punch there and you're sick and dizzy for hours, if not days. So that's where Jack Reacher lands his takedown blow – the side of the head – rather than socking his assailant on the jaw.

Next, Lee Child's hero opts not to use his fists. Again, there's research behind this surprising decision not to follow the staple form of male conflict, the fistfight. In real life, the hand is made up of many small, fragile bones, each one crucial to normal function. Around this collection of tiny, precision components is arranged the greatest concentration of nerves in the human body. Our hands are our primary food-acquiring mechanisms, so have consequent complexity built-in.

Punching someone with your fist, therefore, involves risking serious injury to fragile yet critical components of your everyday functioning. Plus it will hurt, blurring judgement and reaction-time through the first critical seconds of a streetfight. So Jack Reacher uses the big heavy bone in his elbow when he wants to put an adversary out for the count – or the big heavy bone in his brow-ridge, or the big heavy boots he wears – never his fragile hands.

So forget that fistfights have been a staple of tough-guy TV, movies and thrillers for a century. When Jack Reacher first took down a massive opponent with an elbow to the ear, not a sock on the jaw, Lee Child overturned the rules of engagement, and earned a huge amount of respect from his readers. Here was a guy who actually knew the low-down skinny about street-fighting, it seemed. Maybe he'd even been in a few himself.

He may indeed have been, but in an interview Lee Child spilled the beans – he'd found this particular detail in a book about nineteenth-century bare-knuckle prizefighters. Not your obvious reading-material, but Child achieves powerful effects in his work by using facts to turn the stock-in-trade of rough'n'tough thrillers around, and create surprise, authenticity and impact.

In another early Jack Reacher novel, he takes on a tried-and-tested setpiece of tough-guy stories: Russian Roulette. The hero is challenged to a game by the villain, and a revolver is loaded with a single bullet. Fearlessly Reacher picks up the gun, spins the barrel, puts it to his temple and pulls the trigger. *Click.*

Then he spins the barrel again, puts the muzzle to his skull again, and pulls the trigger once more. *Click* again. He does it over and over and over again, staring the villain in the eye, and each time the hammer comes down on an empty chamber. The law of probability says that, with a six-shot revolver loaded with a single shell, six spins of Russian Roulette should result in at least one death. Reacher spins and fires again and again, but each time: *Click.*

Once more, Child uses research to create surprise. We can't believe that each time Reacher puts the gun to his head and triggers it nothing happens. But it does, many times over, seemingly regardless of the laws of probability. Then the author tells us why.

A modern revolver is a precision instrument. Each component is exactly machined and balanced. Fill the revolver with bullets and that balance is perfectly maintained. But put a single shell in, leaving five of the chambers empty, and suddenly the barrel is out of whack. The heavy, loaded chamber will always wind up at the bottom after a random spin, thanks to gun-oil and gravity. The hammer fires on the top chamber. So, given a well-made revolver, Russian Roulette is literally a loaded game.

Try it now

Consider these three familiar action-thriller situations:

* A bomb planted by the villains comes complete with a digital display to show the hero exactly how much time is left.
* When a man and a woman are being pursued on foot, the woman falls and is helped up by the man (unless they're drug addicts, in which case the man falls and is helped up by the woman).
* Villains armed with heavy automatic weapons fire hundreds of rounds at the hero from ten yards away without winging him. The hero, armed with just a lightweight handgun, then picks off each villain as they run with a single shot each.

Now subvert the expectations these arouse. For example, the bomb display could count down from 40 seconds to 20 in the normal way, with the hero battling to defuse it. Then at 19 the countdown disappears and the display flashes 'too late cop'. Think of ways to turn around the expectation created by the cliché you've identified. Now turn to some of the stock, but necessary, scenes in a thriller – the moment where the hero becomes involved in the story, for example. How can you turn around familiar expectations here?

Twists: how thriller authors create whiplash 'reversals'

The Russian Roulette scene generated a powerful reversal of fortunes in Lee Child's novel. From a position of absolute powerlessness in the plot, here was the hero spitting in the villain's eye in every metaphoric way imaginable. Not only was he saying *I'm tougher than you* as he raised the gun to his head for the umpteenth time, smiling as he pulled the trigger. He was also saying to the villain, *you're an amateur: Don't mess with the big boys.*

So, in taking one of the chestnuts of tough-guy fiction and putting it to work, Child created a memorable scene. It both massively increased the reader's respect for him as an author, and cranked up the conflict in his book to a formidable height. Lee Child hasn't mentioned in any interviews where he read about Russian Roulette. There's a reason for that, I think: he didn't read about it. I think he figured it out for himself, using a writer's good sense, and I think it went down like this: Guns are made very carefully; if they're not, they jam. That's a fact anyone can get from the most basic research into firearms. The last thing gun-users want is for their weapon to jam. So guns are pieces of precision engineering.

Research done. The next step is to *apply* the research. In this case, Lee Child thought about what that precision engineering means. He figured-out that misloading a precision revolver, using a single shell instead of half a dozen, will result in the balance of the barrel shifting out of whack. From that deduction, he worked up a brilliant scene which surprises and enlightens us – a solid 'twist'.

Key idea

Twists lead a reader's expectation in one direction before reversing that expectation with a striking actuality. Research is the cornerstone of good twists, and no thriller author mindful of their craft neglects it – approached creatively, research can be a rewarding phase of writerly development in itself.

Lee Child created his Russian Roulette twist by following-through his research into life-or-death facedowns, focusing in on a classic staple of tough-guy stories and going deep beneath the surface. By examining what actually happens in a gun during Russian Roulette, right down to the immutable laws of physics, Lee Child devised a surprising and gripping scene, which in turn performed an important function in his plot – Reacher's superior knowledge of revolvers showed the first hint of weakness in his as yet all-powerful villain. Here was the leader of an armed-to-the-teeth terrorist paramilitary, trounced by a powerless prisoner's superior expertise. The story was set, with a brilliant twist, on a one-way trajectory towards showdown.

Working with reader expectation: 'common sense' versus 'reality'

In both the examples above – the Russian Roulette and the thump on the ear – common sense says one thing and the author says another. In both cases common sense is wrong and the author is right.

Common sense says that a punch in the face is worse than a punch on the ear. Our faces are very sensitive to touch – our ears, not so much. It seems to stand to reason, then, that a blow to the face will be disabling, whereas a wallop on the ear can be shrugged off. But as we've seen, the facts say otherwise.

Common sense says that if a six-shooter has one bullet loaded, then spinning the barrel, putting it to your temple and pulling the trigger six times ought to result in death, probably long before that sixth spin. Except, out in the real world, it doesn't either.

This is the value of in-depth research. You can lead your reader to expect one outcome, based on common sense and the stock-in-trade of mainstream fictions, then surprise them with what actually happens in real life. Because 'common sense' is mostly supposition and wishful thinking; where *savoir faire* is based on fact, common sense is based on fudge. Research gives you savvy. It gives you something the reader hasn't got, because it's your job to have it.

'Savvy' means knowing how to do things. This is why we respect good authors; they know how things go down out there, or seem to. 'Author' as a word is closely related to 'authority'.

Authority is often confused for 'office' these days, but its true meaning is to do with knowledge.

If you want to be an author, seek out facts and soak them up like a sponge baked in a kiln. And if you want to be sure they're facts, not fudge, get them from experts: from the horse's mouth, wherever humanly possible. Use books as your primary source; they're where experts put the good stuff, and always have been.

Practical exercise: getting ideas and generating story

Many successful thrillers start with what writers call a 'what-if' moment. These happen when you're thinking about a situation, or gazing at something, and you think *what if?*

It's important to remember that all the best 'what-if' moments occur while you're negotiating heavy traffic or walking into an important job interview. So the first really critical thing to do is remember your 'what-if' moments. Don't let your mind track back to the task in hand without rejoicing inwardly – these moments are money in the bank to novelists – and storing it for examination at the next available opportunity. If you need to scrawl on your hand to remember your 'what-if', or ask whoever you're with to remind you of a couple of keywords when things are less hectic, then go ahead. These moments are the bread and butter of your creativity, and every single one will merit further thought.

The trick to generating story ideas from 'what-ifs' is to escalate your initial 'what-if' idea, powering it up to transform it from an everyday quirky thing to an event which can trigger or fuel a thriller. Most everyday situations need some pressures applied to them, if they're to grow in dramatic potential. So, for example, a thoughtlessly parked car can generate a whole range of 'what-ifs' by tweaking the circumstances.

For example, a badly-parked car could be blocking the door of a funeral parlour, preventing a funeral from setting off on time, or stopping a corpse being delivered. Both could have novel-length consequences. In this case, the 'what-if' thought process has escalated like this:

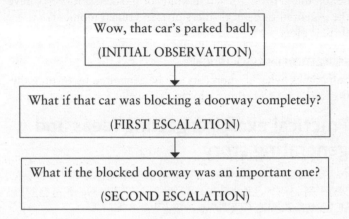

The opening situation of a badly parked car is escalated twice here. In the *first escalation*, the car is not just inconveniencing other people, it's preventing a doorway from being used. The *second escalation* makes the doorway important.

ESCALATION BY LOGICAL EXTENSION

Now the task is to find the kind of doorway whose blocking can create most potential for thriller-style consequences. Firstly, we want to block that door completely – a van is better than a car. And an emergency van is the best kind of van for this situation – a plumber's van, a glazier's – someone who has a reason to be there, and may have a reason to have parked hurriedly, eliminating the need for set-up of any kind.

Now, what kind of everyday doorway is important? What kind of doorway-blocking can have thriller-style consequences? A walk along the service alleys of any retail district will show you all kinds of possibilities. The fortified back door to a bank might be the only way out for employees once the front is locked down for the night; the possibilities in a heist or kidnap heist are self-evident. The back door to a funeral parlour might be the only way to bring corpses in or out, holding up a mobster's funeral, or sending a VIP's body to the wrong depot and getting it lost. All kinds of blocked doorways have the potential to open thrillers or turn crucial moments in thriller plots.

ESCALATION BY ASSOCIATION

Sometimes 'what-if' moments can be generated by turning the first idea into something a lot more fruitful for original story:

> That old hotel looks creepy. What if it was haunted? What if it was *possessed*?

This particular kind of escalation is an *escalation by association*. The *haunted* 'what-if' moment takes on an awesome new power when *haunted* is changed to *possessed*, simply by thinking about what kinds of *haunted* there are.

So, running with the 'possessed hotel' idea for a moment, develop it a little by thinking about how you'd start to plan a novel about a demonic hotel. Questions like:

> When would this story be set for best effect?

In the hotel business, the time of year dictates the kind of people who'll be around. A tourist hotel may be full all summer but empty all winter. It might even close. So is it better to have almost no one around, in this story, or lots of people?

The former, is the obvious answer. The kind of events you'd need for such a story, ones which will make the protagonist blink and think 'did that happen or am I going crazy', wouldn't stand out if the place was hectic and busy, and it would be difficult to rule out human agency in whatever happened. So this story should be set out of season, when the hotel's closed and only a janitor and his family are resident. As you can see, it's only a few short steps from 'That hotel looks kinda creepy...' to Jack Nicholson yelling 'Here's Johnny!' in the movie of Stephen King's supernatural thriller *The Shining*.

Try it now

Schedule a couple of hours next time you've a Saturday morning free (if you can't make Saturdays, a weekday morning). Head with a notebook to where people are, and observe: try your nearest shopping centre, or a bus or railway station, or wherever you're likely to see lots of people.

Start picking out people or situations which catch your eye, and jot down a couple of brief lines about what you've seen and why you've picked up on it. Fill several pages with observations if you can, then start picking ones with 'what-if' potential.

Back at your desk, cherry-pick the jottings that are most interesting to you as you read them. Take a fresh sheet for each, and head the page with a summary of what you jotted down in each instance. Boil it down to the elements which caught your interest.

Now try to use logical and then associative escalation methods on each, as described above. Don't worry about pinning things down with the right words, just record your thoughts as you let your mind make logical or associative connections.

Take your time, and come back to this exercise a few times if you find you're stuck on one or the other – some people find logical connections easy to make, some can associate till the cows come home. But chances are that when both kinds of connections start coming to mind they'll come thick and fast, so have two different pens ready, or a pen and a pencil – one for recording logical escalations, one for recording associative. When you've filled some space on most of your sheets start thinking around your choices. Would these kind of events be good to start a novel? Or turn a key event? Remember, promoting 'what-if' thinking involves some 'blue sky' thinking, so take the time to relax and free your mind from everyday stresses if you find this kind of brain-mode hard to get into.

So far we've looked at the principal tools a thriller writer uses. In the next chapter, we'll study the cogs, gearwheels and pistons of thrillers – components like heroes, villains, twists, triggers and face-offs. First, let's take a moment to recap some key thoughts.

Focus points

Great ideas are made, not born. They come from methodical work, not lightning-bolt inspiration.

Novelists train their minds to sift data and generate ideas by reading widely. Get into the habit of reading as much quality writing as you can, on any subject.

Great twists come from in-depth research. Look specifically for instances where facts seem to contradict 'common sense'. The latter drives readers' expectations; twists turn it around with reality.

Good stories are designed to be compelling and involving; news events aren't. Read the news for insights into how criminals and law enforcement operate, but remember that ideas designed specifically to create dynamic story will always work better on the page than a plot 'borrowed' from real events.

Get in the habit of thinking around situations you see or read about until you can find a 'what-if' point of entry.

Thrillers: Vital Components

In this chapter you will learn:

- ► *How thriller authors create memorable heroes and bone-chilling villains*
- ► *How to light the fuse on an explosive plot*
- ► *What twists are, and how they work*
- ► *How great thrillers build satisfying showdowns*

So far, we've explored the basics of thriller writing, the things an author needs to tackle the challenge of writing a full-length thriller. We've looked at research, and how authors create ideas and twists by applying it; we've investigated using real-world events for fictional purposes; we've looked at how to make space in a busy life to write. These are the basic tools of the craft.

Now let's move on to the engine, the cogs and pistons and driveshafts. In this chapter we'll look in detail at the essential thriller components:

▶ The *protagonist*, or hero/heroine

▶ The *antagonist*, or villain

▶ The all-important *conflict* between the two, which drives the story forward

▶ The *trigger* for an explosive thriller

▶ The *twists*, which create and resolve edge-of-seat moments through a thriller

▶ The satisfying *showdowns* which complete good thrillers

The thriller hero: a case-study analysis

Let's flash back a few decades, to a very different era. It's 1974, just after the Watergate scandal and the OPEC oil crisis, and just as the USA retreats from unthinkable defeat in Vietnam. The world order, seemingly set in stone by two world wars and the rock'n'roll years of boom-time capitalism, has been shaken to its foundations.

Now the extinction of our species – tomorrow, next week, in the next ten minutes – is at stake. The Soviet Union has countless nuclear warheads locked and loaded, enough to annihilate every living thing many times over. The Western powers have equal nuclear capacity, primed similarly for all-out planetary destruction. If anyone hits the red button, for any reason, humanity has a few minutes left.

Yet somehow, from the Cuban Missile Crisis to the fall of the Berlin Wall, though flare-ups came almost incessantly, the missiles stayed in their silos. Again and again, Armageddon seemed imminent if not immediate; yet again and again the world woke up to another day. But behind closed doors, in the most secret of professions, battle raged incessantly, fought by people whose job it was – come hell or high water – not to lose this mother of all face-offs.

Some situations are so dire that only storytellers can really engage with them. The state of world affairs in 1974 was one such. Step up a storyteller equal to the task: John le Carré, a guy who knew about this war because he'd fought on its frontlines himself. His creation, George Smiley, is a warrior at the gates of Armageddon – and one of the most venerated thriller heroes of all time.

THE HERO: STRENGTH

The most enduring thriller protagonists tend to be super-tough. James Bond, for example, who can win any gunfight, or car duel, or ski chase, or speedboat battle. Or, at the other end of the scale, Clarice Starling, a rookie Fed fresh from the academy, facing-down a uniquely lethal criminal in Thomas Harris' Hannibal Lecter series.

Sometimes the hero's toughness is partly in the mind. James Patterson's Alex Cross and Lee Child's Jack Reacher are characterized with high levels of mental discipline, making them sharp strategists as well as hard-man heroes.

But sometimes the toughness of a powerful hero is all in the mind. One of the most memorable thriller heroes of all time – fighting the mother of all battles, with all human life at stake – is a short, fat guy of retirement age. He's thin on top, wears drab suits and raincoats, and can't see without thick spectacles. If his world-stage battles get particularly hellish, he's known to polish his specs on the end of his necktie while he mulls things over.

Remember this

Big battles don't necessarily need big tough guys. The bigger the stakes in a thriller, the greater the proportion of mental versus physical strength needed in the hero.

When George Smiley is not directing global power-plays, with our planet's very future on the line, he reads eighteenth-century German poetry, for fun. He's unlucky in love and given to taking long soul-searching walks. His weapons in the worst face-off in planetary history are a dying, alcoholic, lesbian professor-turned-spy named Constance – Connie for short – plus a few 'lamplighters' and 'street-artists' and other specialist secret agents. When author John le Carré introduces his hero in *Tinker Tailor Soldier Spy*, his setting is a wet winter street in the choking heart of London. He uses a rainstorm to make Smiley seem both ridiculous and a little sad.

The spymaster is shown soaked to the skin, buffeted by a blustery gale as he hurries to a meeting. His drab yet expensive bureaucrat's clothes are unsuited to bad weather, and his paunch makes the sodden cloth yet more cumbersome. The fact that he goes bareheaded in the rain is used to tell us that his beautiful wife has left him many times, on the last occasion ridiculing how silly he looks in winter headgear now he's gone to fat. Consequently his thick glasses are getting the brunt of the rain, and he's forced to walk with his head at absurd angles to drain the deluge from his thick spectacles.

As his hero hurries through the downpour, the verb the author uses to describe his gait isn't 'strode' or even 'trudged', but 'scuttled'. It's a verb usually applied to beetles. This is not your average hero's introduction.

But George Smiley is no average hero. He's the guy who's somehow got to keep the peace, back in the Cold War days of MAD ('mutually-assured destruction', as the global nuclear stand-off was matter-of-factly described), when the entire fate of humanity was on the line.

So John le Carré needed a very human hero. He gave the world George Smiley, an ageing out-of-shape pen-pusher plodding along a rain-soaked street, and millions of readers responded to his classic 'Karla' trilogy. To many, thrillers aside, the Smiley novels are some of the finest literary achievements of the last century.

Part of the reason for this is – just the same as with the Russian Roulette duel discussed in the previous chapter – there's a big twist with Smiley. And, just like the revolver roulette, it comes from knowing what you're writing about. And John le Carré had fought on the Cold War frontlines himself. He knew who the true warriors were in that ultimate battle.

At the gates of Armageddon, in the depths of the Cold War, these warriors were drab-seeming, deskbound government employees. Men and women who were doing the job because they'd been doing it for a very long time. They may have begun their careers dodging bullets behind the lines, but step-up to the top table and you work from HQ. The big bosses live in the suburbs, catch the commuter-trains, and eat lunch in the office cafeteria. Bosses like George Smiley, soaked to the skin and scuttling along a windswept street with his specs fogged up.

Try it now

Designing a fresh and original thriller hero is all about working with thriller readers' expectations, and subverting them in an intriguing way:

* **Jack Reacher** is a big tough guy with expert knowledge of vehicles and weapons, but he doesn't drive a super-charged V12 with RPGs bolted to the chassis – he rides the Greyhound bus or hitches, and the only tool he's packing is a disposable toothbrush.
* **George Smiley** must keep a hostile and murderous superpower in check, but he's thirty years older than Bond and carrying thirty more inches around the waist.

The heroes whom thriller readers respond to most carry big 'reversals of expectation' in their character design.

Try some blue-sky thinking about protagonists. For each of the following thriller scenarios, think of the standard-issue Hollywood kind of hero, and sketch out their character traits until you can make a bullet-pointed list. Now use the traits of the cliché, 'reversing' some and accentuating others, to devise an original, unexpected kind of hero:

* A nuke has been planted in a seismic fault offshore of a Chinese reactor. When it's detonated, the ensuing tsunami will cause a Chernobyl-scale meltdown and crash the global economy.

* A serial killer's victims are carefully stuffed with preserving herbs, rather than dismembered and dissolved in drums of acid.
* A mining corporation pays a cocaine baron to evict native tribes from a metals-rich area.

When you're done, look at the decisions you made with your original list of traits – note which ones you worked with, and which of those proved most tractable or couldn't be changed. You'll see a pattern, of core traits which all thriller heroes need to go the distance, but also of secondary traits, whose purposeful deployment can respin the entire presentation of a protagonist. The key to devising original heroes – and original adversaries – is in creating opportunities for these story-elements to ignite on the page in tension, friction and action.

THE THRILLER VILLAIN: A CLOSE-UP STUDY

George Smiley's adversary, in the mother of global face-offs, is his opposite number in Moscow. A lethal footsoldier, risen through the ranks – and alternately promoted, denounced and tortured, then promoted again by his paranoid superiors – to become boss of the notoriously ruthless Russian secret-service, the KGB.

When this guy frowns, people die. He's the most merciless and fearsome of strategists. Because if he wasn't, he'd be dead himself. He is known only by a codename: Karla. The whisper is, it was the name of his first network of secret-agents, murdered when he himself was jailed and tortured.

He's a formidable antagonist. As the first book in the Smiley series opens, he's just proved to his Western foes that they are losing the battle. Just as, in life, the KGB ran double agents in the very heart of their enemies' secret services, so in the George Smiley thrillers Moscow has won a similar victory – at first.

Protagonist and antagonist in this classic thriller series face-off on both the biggest stage and on the most intimate. Smiley and Karla have met only once, decades before. As a junior Soviet agent, Karla was compromised and arrested briefly in India. Smiley was flown there to persuade him to turn traitor, and defect to the West.

In their sole, short meeting Smiley tries to help the man who will, decades later, become his arch enemy. At the time, both men understand the gravity of the situation. As a junior agent arrested by the enemy, Karla is finished. His presence in this Indian jail makes him a dead man. And it will be far from an easy death, both Karla and Smiley know that for certain. The hero lays it out, working joe to working joe.

Smiley tries to persuade Karla to choose life instead. Sign up with the Western powers; trade his professional knowledge with people who value it, for a new identity and a pension. George Smiley takes a very practical approach to the problem Karla faces.

He even brings some cigarettes, to help Karla think. The only detail known about this young spymaster is that he chain-smokes American cigarettes. Smiley has brought Karla's preferred brand to the interrogation. But though the young Russian has been locked deep inside a roasting Indian prison for several days, with nothing but blood-spattered shirt and pants to call his own, he refuses the offered cigarette.

Refuses everything, in fact. To talk, or react in any way to what's being said. He sits, relaxed, neutral, staring into space. It's a scene between two working joes. Because Karla is at work, as much as Smiley, in this brilliant scene. He's a soldier who's been captured, so his job is not to talk to the enemy. He refuses to respond in any way, all the time Smiley is offering him a lifeline, a chance to avert what will certainly be a horrible death. Karla doesn't flicker an eyelid.

John le Carré didn't need to do anything else to make his villain – the antagonist to his hero – uniquely chilling. Karla is a soldier. Imminent, mortal pain and agonizing death are just part of the job. We don't see him again, not till the closing lines of *Smiley's People*, the last novel in the trilogy. But in the second book, *The Honourable Schoolboy*, Smiley hangs the only known picture of Karla on the office wall at HQ.

It's not much of a portrait. A passport photograph, enlarged on a primitive copier. Smiley has hung it in his office because Karla has made the battle personal. Most thrillers 'make it personal', but le Carré achieves this escalation of conflict in a viscerally nuanced way, making Smiley at times a moving as well as compelling hero to root for.

When Smiley hangs the portrait on his wall, he does so amidst the wreckage of battle lost. He's just uncovered a Soviet agent at the heart of Western intelligence. Many have been murdered or ruined through the course of this betrayal, and even Smiley has been compromised in his search for the traitor.

Because Karla instructed the double agent, working alongside Smiley at the Western top table, to have an affair with Smiley's wife. A messy, indiscreet affair, rubbing the veteran spymaster's nose in it.

Bill Haydon, the betrayer, is not just Smiley's co-worker but his oldest friend. Karla instructed him to cuckold his colleague so that Smiley – an honourable, ethical man, as well as a masterspy alert to treason – would doubt his own judgement when it came to Haydon.

Key idea

In a thriller, the villain must be powerfully engaged with the hero, so that conflict plays out on multiple levels. This opens up opportunities for building depth and drama from unexpected sources page-by-page through the course of a gripping thriller.

Le Carré's big twist here is a nice development of something that went down the first, and only, time we're shown Karla in close-up. Because back in the depths of the Indian prison, when his life was on the line, Karla refused Smiley's cigarettes – his brand of choice, too – but he stole his lighter.

Again, a soldier in the field. In the Indian prison, Karla has nothing but a shirt and pants in his possession, and a high-security jail to escape from. A butane lighter is a useful acquisition to a guy in this position. As it turns out, Karla doesn't use it to escape. He refuses to talk to the Brits or the Indians, and is eventually released. Soviet secret agents grab him at the prison gates, and he's bundled back to Moscow, tortured within an inch of his life – only to turn the tables, and become in time the man who orders torture. What kind, how much, and for whom.

So in plot terms, the stolen lighter is a dead end. But, in story terms, the author uses it to make a single, mostly silent encounter resonate through three entire thrillers.

The stolen lighter was a gift from Smiley's yet-to-be-unfaithful wife. Engraved to him, with love. In the Indian jail, Karla palms it. Decades later, he instructs Smiley's oldest friend to cuckold him, and make sure Smiley knows about it. To cloud Smiley's judgement, to make the traitor the very last guy Smiley will allow himself to suspect. To occlude the spymaster's vision – remember that very first glimpse of Smiley, in a blinding rainstorm with his spectacles fogged up?

At the start of the second book in the 'Karla' trilogy, the subterfuge has worked, right up until the moment Smiley unmasked it. Now the West is severely compromised in its fight against nuclear devastation.

Smiley's first move in the counterstrike is to brief a hand-picked agent for a high-stakes mission. Smiley's right-hand enforcer joins him for a tense meeting with the agent, Jerry. Briefing over, and mission accepted, Jerry considers the enemy's blurry portrait, hung in pride of place at HQ.

Jerry is a soldier about to go to the frontline trenches. 'Karla', the KGB boss in the photo, will in all probability be torturing Jerry to death in the coming weeks. So he jokes about the portrait, saying that Karla's poker-face makes him look like he's got a rectal blockage; earthy folk-humour surprises the reader into snickering aloud despite the tension.

Both men know very well the mettle of this guy, and what it will mean for them personally in the skirmishes to come. So everything they say – like soldiers in the field, about to face battle – is a mocking put-down of their enemy. It's a funny yet moving scene.

But this exchange of banter in front of a blurry, grainy portrait is our last glimpse of Karla, the villain of this trilogy of novels, right up to the closing seconds of the final showdown. Smiley hangs the picture early in the second book, with battle about to commence – for the rest of its action, and all but the last lines of the third novel, Karla is not on the page.

An incredible achievement. For the entirety of his globally bestselling thriller trilogy, John le Carré fleshed out one of the most venerated villains in literary history using just what his hero might have in the real world – nothing but a faded photograph, a long-ago memory of a silent condemned man, and a stolen, sentimentally engraved cigarette lighter.

Triggers: igniting a thriller

A story's triggering event is easy to spot. It's where the story shifts into gear and gets moving.

Key idea

A trigger is the scene in a thriller which changes the status quo, apparently for ever – so that normality can't be restored without heroic effort from the protagonist.

The most explosive thrillers hit the ground running. The action kicks off almost immediately: often in the first few scenes. The author doesn't want to waste any time, to get the adrenalin pumping and keep it there. Action-thriller novelists need to use all the big opportunities for drama that are available over the course of a novel, so they get moving fast. Stakes are raised very quickly, and the action turns deadly very soon.

All triggers ignite the action; some direct its nature. In Elmore Leonard's *Rum Punch*, filmed by Tarantino as *Jackie Brown*, an over-the-hill air hostess is caught at Miami International smuggling a weight of cash for a gun-runner. The hostess has a prior, carrying coke for a pilot twenty years ago, so now she is royally screwed.

On the one hand, she has ATF agents who can put her in jail for much of what's left of her life; on the other, she has a heavyweight gangster who urgently wants her dead. So this trigger invokes dual foes and dual dilemmas: Jackie Brown's solution, as a resourceful independent woman, is to sting them both, playing one foe against the other, and escaping with the ill-gotten gains.

'Trigger' incidents shift the story into *drive*. The status quo is interrupted, and something the protagonist values is put at stake. The balance of life is disrupted until they can restore it.

In thriller fiction, as we learned in the first chapter, the jeopardy in the story will be pushed to the end of the line in the process. To set things right, the hero must go all out and all the way. Cue the most powerful component of the thriller:

Conflict: battles and wars

The conflict of a thriller animates the face-off between hero and villain. It can incorporate skirmishes, battles, brinksmanship and all-out war.

Planning such conflict is a daunting task for any writer attempting a thriller. There's a lot of action and white-knuckle suspense to deliver over the course of a full-length story. A browse through bestselling thrillers will show anyone that these novels contain dozens of high-octane scenes at the very least. It's a lot for a budding thriller writer to come up with.

Fortunately this is where our toolbox gets really useful. Central to any novelist's skill set is an understanding of *drama* and its uses in fiction. This helps thriller writers build the conflict of their novels, using *dramatic structure* to decide:

▶ what kind of conflict they need

▶ what it will put at stake

▶ where, when and how it should go down in the story

▶ how high-octane it should be

▶ who should win – hero or villain, protagonist or antagonist

▶ what the victory triggers.

Dramatic structure is the framework which builds stories. Even the stories we hear as little kids, even fairy stories, follow strict dramatic structure.

Most stories have three dramatic *acts*. Acts are sequences of scenes that build, one on another, to crescendos of action and suspense.

These crescendos are the *act climaxes* and *mid-act climaxes*. They do what the name says. They climax the action of each, escalating series of scenes or scene sequences. They provide the big twist or face-off that slingshots the story into its next phase.

Key idea

Dramatic structure sounds technical but, when planning a novel, it's an easy tool to use. A three-act thriller needs three act climaxes and three mid-act climaxes. Six big infusions of energy into the story. Six powerful crescendos.

So planning the conflict of a thriller breaks down quite simply on paper. You need to devise six big turning-points for the story. Each must escalate the jeopardy – what's at stake in the story – until the final climax.

So to begin you need six sequences of scenes, to set up each of the six climaxes. Breaking it down on paper makes it a simple flowchart process. The kind of action you choose derives from your choices of hero and villain. The world of the story is wherever their opposition can create most friction.

What each crescendo of the story – each act climax and mid-act climax – must do above all else is slingshot the story forward. We call these slingshot moments 'twists'. And to many, writers and fans alike, they're the most inspirational components of thriller fiction.

Twists

Readers love great twists in thrillers – those dizzying yet powerful reversals of fortune, which scupper heroes and leave villains riding high. Or, as in the Russian Roulette twist described above, give a hero some psychological traction against an all-powerful villain.

To a reader they're 'twists'; but to a thriller writer they're set-ups and pay-offs. Remember the moment in *The Usual Suspects* where Kevin Spacey suddenly stops limping, and starts striding down the street? A powerful twist, a final-act climax which repositions the entire story as set-up to this final pay-off. In doing so it reveals that the guy we thought was just a minor thief, a loser with a bad case of verbal diarrhoea, was the big Kahuna all along. A great twist.

Key idea

Knockout twists are moments of genius, so trying to think up ideas for them can be daunting. Yet, as with much of the challenge of writing thrillers, the big twists come not from lightning-bolt inspiration, but from storycraft.

Twists in a thriller tend to cluster around the climaxes – in a standard three-act structure there will be six big climaxes. Three mid-act climaxes building to three act climaxes.

So professional novelists plan a thriller by deciding who's going to 'win' each climax. The story's not going to be plain sailing for the hero, of course, so some of the climaxes will be victories for the villain. An alternating pattern is the basic template – a mid-act climax which leaves the hero scuppered may be followed by an act climax where the hero turns the tables. Or, if things are really tough, both of an act's big climaxes might go against the hero, forcing them to dig deep in order to fight back in the next act. If it's a particularly gruelling battle, with something especially worth fighting for at stake, the hero might not 'win' a climax until the final movement of the novel.

From these simple beginnings, great thrillers are born. Because once we have a rough idea of our six crescendos, we can begin to design scene sequences that will build up to them. It's in these sequences that we'll sow the seeds of the decisive factors in each climax – the sharp edge the villain can get over the hero, the unsuspected traction the hero can exert in the unlikeliest place. These sown seeds will flourish into the climaxes and twists of the story, all the way to the final face-off.

Showdowns

Much of the money spent in Hollywood goes on showdowns. Screen stories, delivered visually, need big visual pay-offs. Everyone can picture a classic movie showdown – the epic battles that fill screens with gunfire and explosions and smoking wreckage.

But novels, where the story is narrated, can work showdowns very differently. Suspense and tension are psychological in nature, so thriller novels often crank these aspects of a showdown as much as the pyrotechnics. Think of the ending of *The Silence of the Lambs*, or its sequel *Hannibal*. The latter has one of the goriest climaxes ever – a villain is made to eat his own brain, whilst still alive – but dialogue, replete with darkest irony, is the real meat of the scene.

Which isn't to say that thrillers shouldn't end in explosions. Action thrillers typically climax with all-out physical conflict. The hero functions as a one-man army in scenes brimming with ingenious tactical twists, and replete with a true soldier's courage under fire.

But sometimes, even in high-octane thrillers, powerful outcomes can be achieved without pyrotechnics. T. C. Boyle's novel *Talk Talk*, a thriller about identity theft, is one long cross-country chase, California to New York. The villain is a sophisticated career-criminal, the hero is a deaf woman. The showdown is a foot-chase through crowded city streets – the big twist here is that, even on the fly, the villain manages to paint his speech-disabled adversary as a crazy woman running amok. He even enlists passing cops to help him escape her.

Yet she doesn't give up, and remains in hot pursuit until the breathless showdown comes. The villain has the heroine cornered. We cringe in anticipation of what he's going to do to her. She can't even scream for help.

Then the author surprises us. We're expecting a blade to appear from nowhere, a gun to materialize in the villain's hand. Worse, we fear there'll be no knife or gun, and that this villain will exact payback with his fists.

But here's where the author's hard work pays off. Throughout the story, Boyle has built his villain as a guy who steals so he can look cool. He's a thief, but he's also a *haute-cuisine* chef, a connoisseur of fine wines and prestige cars, a clotheshorse. He's spent his whole life creating an image, one that will make women look at him in a certain way. With wide, impressed, come-hither eyes.

Boyle uses this character work to power an extraordinary showdown. Cornered by the villain, the deaf woman has only one weapon. She can't shout for help; she can't get into a fistfight and hope to win. But she can use her eyes. So the heroine gives the thief one long, frank look. A woman who has had to fight for everything in her life, gazing in contempt at a cheat who steals whatever he wants.

And it's all she needs to do. The villain wilts. Deflates and slinks away, utterly defeated by the knowledge of what a substandard human being he is. For years he's stolen ordinary people's hard-earned cash, to keep up the pretence that he's a successful man. One withering look from an honest woman shatters the false reality he's built for himself, and he's finished.

It's a powerful and satisfying climax to a tense chase story, delivered without a single gunshot. Not even a sucker-punch. Satisfying dramatic resolution is generated from the most basic of human interactions – eye contact – in this masterful thriller showdown. Less is more, indeed.

Try it now

Showdowns are sequences where a reader's expectation must be led in one direction and then be 'reversed', repeatedly, creating cascades of surprising developments as fate hangs in the balance.

With each of the following showdown scenarios, isolate the expectation the action arouses, then look at how you can subvert that expectation.
* a car chase, a tinny hatchback versus a two-ton truck
* a villain at bay with a child hostage
* a hero who must get through a border-crossing in a 'hot' vehicle.
Now note the new position you've brought the action to, and the expectations which it provokes in itself, and subvert that with your next move: See if you can create a cascade effect of subverted expectations creating new intriguing drama – this is a core skill of successful thriller authors.

Bringing it all together

We've studied the precision components of the supercharged thriller engine in this chapter – heroes and villains, triggers and showdowns, conflict and twists. We've used narrative know-how to break each of these down into manageable authorial choices – the set of decisions that all writers make through the planning stage of a novel. We've explored the rules, and seen that sometimes rules exist to be broken.

Now we're going to examine these thriller components in detail, working step-by-step through the choices an author makes when it's time to put ink on the page, and start drafting a thriller. First, let's recap the key ideas to take forward.

Focus points

'Less is more' is a sound principle to follow in your line-by-line writing, but it can also be applied to character design. Look to distil character, not dilute it by packing in features.

Novelists use dramatic structure to design their stories. Understanding it can make the task of sketching a story idea into a fully-realized progression a practical job, not a strain on creativity.

Using a three- or five-act structure will show you where to place the key action, and what it needs to deliver, allowing you to move logically from one high-point to the next in your design.

Big twists don't have to be fiendishly ingenious and complicated – the simple action of a man striding along, where before he limped, makes for one of the biggest twists in thriller history.

Showdowns are a thriller writer's ace in the hole. Unlike movies or TV, with their daunting budgetary demands, the only limits for a novelist are those of the story. But showdowns don't have to be pyrotechnic. In a battle-of-wits thriller, for example, a simple action – freighted with the subtext which the story has taught us to read – can resonate louder than a thousand gunshots.

The Thriller Hero

In this chapter you will learn:

▶ *Which attributes a thriller hero needs to fight to the end of the line*

▶ *How authors create compelling heroes using character and characterization*

▶ *How to design a backstory for a hero that will maximize your story's potential*

▶ *About the different types of hero a thriller can use, and why*

What makes a hero?

Now let's focus in detail on the protagonist, or hero – the human agency which drives the quest of the story. Let's go back a moment to the definition of a thriller:

> A thriller is a mystery which pushes jeopardy to the end of the line.

The hero of a thriller must be someone who is capable of going that distance – all the way. This doesn't mean a hero has to be superhuman, super-fit and super-cool. In our first discussion of heroes we looked at George Smiley. He's out of shape, over the hill, at a rather far distance from 'cool' – yet he's the hero of three of the tensest, biggest-stakes thrillers ever penned.

What all thriller heroes need – if they're to solve the mystery, and fight right up to the end of the line – are attributes to draw on. These might include:

- street smarts
- detective skills
- combat training
- access to technologies (automotive databases, cellphone records, etc.)
- interrogation skills
- wilderness survival know-how.

Amongst others. Enforcement professionals – cops and 'Feds' – have many of the above attributes but are bound by the rules and regulations of the job. This is why thrillers rarely use clock-punching cops as heroes – those rules and regulations limit the protagonist's ability to go credibly 'to the end of the line'. For most working cops, a situation that escalates to deadly jeopardy means they're sidelined, while a tactical-response unit takes over. Mystery novels and whodunnits are the domain of the cop-on-the-job, rarely thrillers.

Yet very few civilians have the kind of attributes listed above, presenting a dilemma to the thriller writer. This conundrum is often solved by using an enforcement professional as protagonist, but removing the rules and regulations that bind them.

Remember this

High-octane thriller plots often demand, from their hero, attributes that civilians can't credibly possess – weapons training, or pursuit-driving skills for example. So many thriller heroes are enforcement professionals, who are 'off the leash' for the action of the story. They can go to the end of the line in a thriller without getting tied up in red tape or disciplinary hearings.

This problem – how to make your hero a cop without a badge, a soldier without a unit – has provoked much creative thinking among thriller authors. Ian Fleming solved it by giving his hero a special 'licence to kill'. James Bond has all the training, technologies and contacts of state enforcement, but is deniable. He's not a public-office holder, like a cop or a soldier – he's a secret agent. The rules of the job are whatever he deems necessary.

Elmore Leonard solved the same problem across many different thrillers by using trained enforcement agents as heroes, but putting them 'off-leash' at the time of the action. In many Leonard novels, the heroes are cops, US Marshals, federal agents – but, when the plot of the book kicks in, they're between postings, or taking a career-break, or suspended from duty for political reasons (i.e. those that don't reflect adversely on the hero's character). They have all the training, tools and contacts of cops, but they're 'off-leash' for the duration of the action.

Lee Child solved the same problem by making his series hero a downsized military cop. Jack Reacher has in-depth knowledge of enforcement and the military, plus advanced combat, survival, and interrogation skills – but now he's his own boss. The military made him a formidable soldier, then it made him unemployed. Now Reacher is answerable to nothing and no one, except his own values.

Some thriller writers go to the other extreme – their heroes are ordinary men and women pushed to extraordinary feats of courage and will by the demands of the plot. In T. C. Boyle's

4. The Thriller Hero

The Tortilla Curtain, the hero is a penniless Mexican 'illegal', living rough in California with his pregnant wife. He knows no one, he has nothing, and the very fact of being in the USA makes him a criminal.

He's hit by a car in the novel's opening lines, and is seriously injured, but can't go to hospital. To seek medical help will invite deportation, and put him right back into the poverty he'd hoped to escape for the sake of his wife and unborn kid. So he toughs it out, though he's sick with pain and passing blood. Things get rougher from there on in.

His camp is trashed by local teens, his scavenged possessions wrecked; his work disappears, and he has to live from what his heavily pregnant wife can earn scrubbing metal with dangerous chemicals. Ultimately his wife is brutally raped and becomes seriously depressed. The couple's one stroke of good fortune, a Thanksgiving turkey given away for free, leads to a wildfire which incinerates their scanty savings. All the hero has, from start to life-or-death finish, is the will to survive. The most basic human trait, fuelling a fine, deeply moving thriller.

Heroes: surface and depth

So can a thriller hero be anyone at all? The answer is yes. Just so long as they are invested in what's at stake in the story, and have the ability – if they dig deep within themselves – to go to the very end of the line.

In the hands of a skilled thriller writer, ordinary people can become extraordinary heroes. This is accomplished by building a powerful contrast between surface and depth in the protagonist's construction.

We can see this technique at work in the hero of *The Tortilla Curtain*. The Mexican is ragged and unkempt, malnourished and desperate. He gets around by trudging along the trash-strewn shoulders of six-lane highways. He's dirty, dressed in grimy rags, and he smells bad. Most of us would cross the street to avoid him. In terms of the pecking order of society, he's right down there with the lowest of the low.

He looks like a hobo. He smells like a hobo. As he waits with the other illegals on a street corner – for a builder or farmer's truck, and a day's cash-in-hand work – the Mexican is worse than a hobo, to the rush-hour traffic streaming past. He's a freeloader, a parasite looking to milk the system without paying a penny in tax.

So the opening of the novel shows us what the protagonist looks like, to the outside world. And he looks like a down-and-out, at best. Not your typical hero at all.

The presentation is so powerful that, at first, readers of this extraordinary thriller are skilfully led to identify instead with the novel's 'antagonist', its villain. This guy is a white American liberal, an eco warrior, a man who has inherited wealth yet writes a humble nature page for a monthly magazine, and spends the rest of his time hiking responsibly, cooking expertly, and caring like a thoroughly modern man for his wife and son. This is the guy who clips the Mexican, in the opening scene, with his car.

The novel that follows shows us the truth behind both surfaces. The grubby illegal immigrant turns out to be nothing more than what he really is – a determined man from a poor background. Someone who's had to live without the benefits of first-world parents, a first-world education and a first-world passport. Someone who grew up in a shack, eating whatever could be coaxed from a patch of hardpan dirt. Someone with toughness at his core. Someone who, no matter how bad things get, refuses to give up. A guy who can go to the end of the line – and Boyle pushes the action to the absolute heart-in-mouth end – yet emerge with his human values intact.

The other guy, the politically correct eco warrior, with his beautiful life and nature writing, turns out to be the hero's opposite. By the time of the novel's shocking conclusion, he's become – brilliantly convincingly – a paranoid one-man vigilante, human values quite forgotten as he patrols what he sees as his territory.

The novel's art is to work this transmutation gradually. And, in doing so, to pose a radical question. Perhaps this affluent white liberal, with his inheritance and luxury house and nature column – perhaps he's the real freeloader, the real parasite. His fear of the poor, and his deeply cached racism, are simmered to a raging boil by the author over the course of a compelling thriller.

The reader is led from the opening position that the American is the character to identify with, and the Mexican a dark representation of the threat of the lawless poor, to a complete polar reversal. Villain and hero transmute, and swap places entirely. It's an amazing feat of writing, achieved by exploiting to its utmost potential one of the ground rules of fiction.

Heroes, villains, and all principals in between, must have a contrast between their *characterization* and their deep *character*. Who they appear to be is not who they really are. James Bond looks like a dilettante playboy. Bond villains look like wealthy philanthropists.

Key idea

It's this contrast between surface and depth, between characterization and true character, that brings heroes and villains to life in novels. In thrillers, novels designed to deliver tense and powerful stories at pace, we push the contrast as powerfully as we can.

Jane Austen exploited this contrast between character and characterization again and again in her classic novels written two centuries ago. Yet, right on the contemporary pulse, blood-and-guts thrillers full of incendiary action and heartstopping suspense use the exact same technique.

Try it now

Choose a thriller which you've particularly enjoyed, and write down the kind of person that the hero is. List the qualities that you as a reader see most in them.

Now turn to the page where that hero is first introduced. What's being emphasized in the author's presentation through these first scenes? What are the 'first impressions' that a reader is given? Write these down, then compare the lists. You'll see the author carefully setting up the contrast between *characterization* and deep *character*, in the differences you've noted.

Character and characterization: using 'backstory'

The *characterization* of the protagonist is who the author needs them to be for the conflict of the novel to kick off.

We've looked at how the hero needs to have certain attributes. These may be nothing more than specialist knowledge of the novel's territory and a moral conscience, in a political or business thriller. In an action thriller it might be firearms training and martial arts expertise.

Such attributes will derive, to an extent, from the hero's history, whether they're a hardened combat vet or a white-collar whistle-blower. Their 'backstory' – all the details of their history that a reader needs to know – will determine the role they play in the novel. The hero will need to inhabit that role credibly through the course of the novel, but *characterization* attributes are factors that are fixed in place when the story starts.

Attributes of *deep character* aren't static. They grow and develop over the course of the novel. They develop from characterization attributes, either reinforcing or subverting them as the hero progresses. They derive from backstory, equally. Let's look at an example of a character with a rich backstory, and examine how it generates energy in the present.

Backstory in action: a case-study analysis

In John Burdett's superlative 'Bangkok' thrillers, the hero is a cop working a tough district of a tough city. To say that he has a challenging job, and conflicted loyalties, is putting it mildly.

His boss is both a distinguished police chief and a top-tier gangster; he combines both roles in his working day. The hero's mother is a high-class prostitute, now retired, owner of one of the busiest bar-girl joints in Bangkok. Traditions of Thai respect dictate that the hero must serve both his boss and his mother in their business activities.

Yet Detective Sonchai Jitpleecheep also solves fiendishly ingenious, unrelentingly horrific murders in one of the world's most vibrant cities – and one of its most corrupt. He's an amazing cop, cerebral yet very human, and very embedded in the down-and-dirty backstreets of Bangkok. That's his *characterization* in this bestselling thriller series.

But the development of his deep *character* takes things way deeper. It achieves this by drawing on the richness of the hero's *backstory*.

Key idea

Backstory isn't just a protagonist's biography. Backstory is composed of the parts of a hero's history which impact the present-day action. It's where the seeds are sown for how – and if – the protagonist will rise to the novel's challenges.

Sonchai's backstory is this: After a childhood flitting around Europe between the grand houses of his mother's clients, back in Bangkok Sonchai ran with a bad crowd who ultimately murdered a drug dealer. His punishment, after his mother paid a hefty bribe to police chief Colonel Vikorn, was to be sent to a Buddhist monastery in the wilds of the Thai jungle.

Here Sonchai received a punishing spiritual education and emerged, with his best friend Pichai, as full-on Buddhist monks. Colonel Vikorn arranged for their rehabilitation, however. Now both young monks must work for him, as both apprentice cops and gangster's gofers, to pay their debt.

Pichai is Sonchai's best friend, spiritual soulmate and co-servant of Vikorn. He's killed, nightmarishly, in the opening scene of *Bangkok 8*, the first thriller in the series. From there on in, in a narrative that's a heady brew of both Asian *savoir faire* in a tough world, and spiritual insight in a karmic odyssey, Sonchai works the blood-spattered frontline of Thai crime. Whilst doing whatever Vikorn's ongoing gangster wars require of him, plus deferring to his mother's needs as a brothel-owner with a cop for a son. With Pichai's ghost looking over his shoulder, to stretch his loyalties even further.

CHARACTER DEVELOPMENT: BACKSTORY IN ACTION

The two people to whom Sonchai is answerable in worldly life –
his boss and his mother – are both intricately involved in his
backstory. Sonchai owes both a powerful debt, yet they're both
primarily involved with illegal activities. And Sonchai is a good-
seeking guy, by vocation and by profession. He's a cop at work,
and a Buddhist the rest of the time.

In the rich design of this backstory, author John Burdett created
a wide variety of opportunities for both boss and mother's
activities to intersect meaningfully with Sonchai's life. This
naturally creates many chances for Sonchai's backstory to be
invoked, and for his deep character to develop through action.
When, after sequences of tough homicide investigation, we
forget that Sonchai has an opposing side to him – the karmic
savant who sees clearly the impermanence of all material things,
particularly human life – Sonchai's mother, or his boss, or his
dead friend's spirit, remind us.

Try it now

Backstory creates pressure and pace in the present tense of a thriller's
unfolding action. How can you flesh out the following backstories, to
open up opportunities in a thriller?

* the head of a murderous secret service is a former psychologist
* a Fed working Organized Crime is the child of a pizza-shop owner
* a frustrated cop misses a chance to dispense actual justice – then
  years later gets another.

In each case, look for opportunities to build contrast between surface and
depth. As you work, consider how surface is something we can control day
to day – depth, however, is built though a lifetime of experience. The key
to devising a fertile backstory is to exploit the energy and dissonance of
that fundamental contrast.

The contrast Burdett creates between his detective hero's
initial *characterization* and his *deep character* is reinforced
repeatedly by a narrative design which dramatizes Sonchai's
characterization – the cop from the wrong side of the tracks –
and invokes his deep character, of a spiritual seeker wrestling
with the knotty paradoxes of Buddhist wisdom.

This permits all kinds of fun in the novels. One rich vein of entertainment – and of professional education for Sonchai – derives from watching Colonel Vikorn in action. Vikorn is a master strategist, a true operator, in both his police-boss and his boss-gangster careers. Scenes where he locks horns with rivals, or defers to more senior operators whilst shaking them down, are a delight to read. We see them through Sonchai's eyes, as he both learns from the master and wrestles with the karmic conundrums that Vikorn's actions generate.

Both sets of consequences resonate for Sonchai, interrogating the question all religions try to answer. *How should we live?* For this hero, policing an ethical ground zero – Bangkok, where East and West collide – complicates matters, intriguingly. His backstory, as a Buddhist monk, teenage tearaway, and grand-a-night hooker's son, is never far from his present-day role as a cop. Backstory is used powerfully to create characterization, and develop true character, in the hero of this vibrant thriller series.

Types of hero

HERO ON THE OUTSIDE: THE 'BIG GUY' PROTAGONIST

The central project of the thriller is to prove that appearances are deceptive. That, whatever's on the outside, the unvanquishable human spirit burns within.

So the characterization of the hero – the façade, from which 'first impressions' arise – is often at powerful odds with the actuality. In thrillers, a bottom-of-the-pile hobo can be a hero.

The classic exploiter of this differential was James Bond's creator, Ian Fleming. On the surface, 007 is a playboy. He hangs out in high-stakes casinos, sips custom-prepared Martinis, skippers both speedboats and yachts with aplomb. Most of us guys look like waiters when we sport a dinner jacket, but Bond's tuxedo is a weapon of mass seduction. A ladies' man, a suave guy.

Behind that slick surface, Bond is an elite special-forces soldier. An intense, super-fit, all-guns-blazing commando, honed by investigative espionage, and given the ultimate licence to kill, this slick lounge-lizard is a deniable secret agent and deadly deep-cover assassin.

Think of an actor from a good screen thriller. Write down how they come across in that movie – physically, personally, professionally. Now put this persona in the world of your story. Keep the actor's face if it helps. What would this character wear, in the world of your story? How would they get around? What would they do for money? Where would their friends be, in this world? List these qualities, then write another column, of the attributes your story needs in its key characters. Start making connections between the two columns, and label them *first impressions* and *deep character*. Before you know it, you'll be fleshing-out the kind of character your story needs.

It's this strong contrast between surface and depth, between characterization and true character, which makes thriller heroes equal to the demands of high-octane plots. But not all thriller heroes are guns-blazing soldiers. Many are regular, working joes caught up in incendiary situations.

THE HERO INSIDE: 'LITTLE GUY' PROTAGONISTS

In John le Carré's recent bestselling thriller *The Mission Song*, the hero is an African living in London. He's a sub-Saharan languages expert, who translates at official interviews with recent arrivals to the UK. One day he's hired for a job that will take all weekend. It turns out to be a top-secret conference between African leaders, from a notoriously war-torn region. The hero is hired to translate at these crucial talks.

It's a prestige assignment but not an unheard-of one. At most international conferences, the delegates don't speak each other's languages. They wear headphones, through which a translator relays what's just been said. The translator works from the conference's audio-control room, surrounded by switchboards.

There are dozens of sound inputs feeding into the translator's headphones, activated automatically when people start speaking. Microphones from the conference room, mikes from the rooms where lunch is eaten and coffee drunk. In *The Mission Song*, the translator's job is to listen to what the delegates are saying, whether they're facing-off over the conference table, or talking aside in a break, and translate it for the conference organizers.

So there are lots of negotiations for the hero to listen in on. Many nuanced inflections to translate. It's a tough assignment for the protagonist, regardless of his own feelings about the fate of his countrymen. There are many microphones feeding into his translator's headphones, often simultaneously, so it's a high-tension, high-performance job of work.

On the second day, during a coffee break, the translator gets a big surprise over the audio. A horrible one. What he hears through his headphones is a delegate being tortured – brutally electrocuted. Shocked, threatened, then shocked again, as he hangs shackled in a hidden room.

The translator recognizes the torturers' voices. They're the guys who hired him. Ten minutes later, the tortured delegate is back at the conference table. Not a hair out of place. The negotiations continue.

This isn't the trigger to the story, but a second-act climax. The story proper kicks in when the translator sees the African delegates to this crucial conference for the first time. Because they're not power-brokers from any war-torn region – these are warlords and chieftans from one of the most economically critical areas of the twenty-first century.

Their strife-torn patch of Africa is the world's only source of certain rare metals: those vital to smartphones and all portable devices. A large part of the global economy – and, for many, a modern lifestyle – depends directly on stability in the troubled region.

And that's what the conference achieves. A peace is brokered. The rare-metal mines will supply the global economy. From dot-com digi-workers in San Francisco to Cambodian villagers with a communal cellphone, people everywhere can continue life as they know it.

But the translator knows how this deal was brokered. He knows every detail of the backhand transactions between the players, and the pressures applied to reach a deal. He knows precisely who will profit from this peace accord, and who will suffer. Can he see his ancestral homeland governed this way? Collect his pay and walk away?

It's a powerful dilemma that drives a whiplash thriller. In *The Mission Song*, John le Carré proved that his power to dramatize the real battles of our times – the ones behind the headlines – remained undiminished, after five decades of bestselling thrillers.

Try it now

What kind of 'little guy' protagonist might the following scenarios deploy?

✳ drug-barons seeking to move their cash from the USA, where their product is sold, to where they can spend it

✳ a terrorist plot to ransom a city

✳ a racist assassin who targets minority community-leaders.

Again, go for the standard-issue idea first, then look at ways of subverting the expectations provoked – allow yourself plenty of lateral thinking as you devise routes to solutions where 'little guys' can prove pivotal.

Little-guy protagonists deliver powerful identification for the reader. The hero is someone just like us. Not a top-level player but an ordinary person, just like us. Or worse off, like the hero of *The Tortilla Curtain*. Such heroes reach deep inside themselves, and find the power to meet extraordinary challenges. To a skilled thriller author, a little-guy protagonist can anchor a vigorous human story.

PARTNERS AND TEAM PLAYERS: MULTIPLE PROTAGONISTS

One particular use of the 'little guy' hero is in dual-protagonist stories. Dual-protagonist stories were pioneered in 'the golden age' of crime fiction – the private-eye yarns of the 1930s and 40s. Freelance detectives, like classic heroes Philip Marlowe and Sam Spade, teamed up with wronged clients to solve mysteries. These 'noir' stories combined an off-leash professional with a wronged client (usually female) in a dual protagonist set-up.

Through the decades that followed, thriller fiction evolved this powerful dynamic, of *dual protagonists*, often using it to show conflict at two levels simultaneously – the little guy on the ground, and the big guy fighting the war at HQ.

Remember this

The utility of the dual-protagonist device, in thrillers about enforcement or espionage campaigns, is wide and fruitful. As a story unfolds in real time, action at ground zero can be undermined or reinforced by the battles back at mission control.

In this kind of thriller, 'dramatic irony' – what the guy on the ground doesn't know, yet – can be deployed powerfully, making readers turn pages with heart-in-mouth as the little guy battles into hidden peril. Or we can watch, equally transfixed, as the big guy puts his own head on the block, to give the guy on the ground a chance to grab victory from the jaws of defeat.

In many crime and espionage thrillers, a little-guy hero is used as one half of a dual-protagonist setup. The second central character is often a senior cop or spymaster. Either they're running an agent as their dual protagonist – be that agent cop or spy – or the second protagonist is a true 'little guy', and the spymaster or senior-cop steps in to help when an ordinary person gets embroiled in a dangerous situation, on their watch. It's a technique that doubles our identification with the hero, by splitting it between dual protagonists.

Our emotional involvement is with the little-guy hero. He's the one we root for in our guts as we read, the guy fighting the battle on the ground. But our will for good to win through is invested in the spymaster, who fights the battle at HQ – where the ultimate stakes are higher and the conflict is most treacherous.

But thrillers are rarely uncomplicated. In Frederick Forsyth's classic *The Dogs Of War*, the dual-protagonist device is used with savage power. Both of Forsyth's dual protagonists are terrible men. One is a seasoned soldier-for-hire. He specializes in regime change, for the benefit of the highest bidder. The fate of ordinary people, the soon-to-be-starving citizens of the countries he storms, is not his concern.

He's the guy on the ground in the novel. Back at HQ, his co-protagonist is a wealthy industrialist, a guy who's got the inside geological dope on a big platinum deposit in central Africa. His plan is to send elite mercenaries into the country that sits over the platinum, and overthrow its government with a violent *coup d'état*. Install a puppet dictator, and sign mining rights over to his own offshore consortium.

A ruthlessly unscrupulous power-broker, teamed with a ruthless killer. Both are far from being 'white knights'. Both are damnably tainted by what they do. The novel was inspired, it's said, by the author's first-hand experience of a terrible African conflict. Forsyth had no illusions about the kinds of scramble going on there in the post-colonial Cold War years.

So he made both his central characters people we disapprove of. Because, in the real world of guns-for-hire and bloody *coups d'état,* there are no sympathetic characters. Such is the masterly novel's implicit message.

Yet over the breakneck course of this thriller, the mercenary's soldierly loyalty to the corps – his own lethal professionalism – transmutes, to function as the force for good. Ultimately he pulls a *coup* that is entirely his own, resolving a deadly serious story with a powerful twist.

Remember this

Thriller protagonists can be quite repugnant in their characterization, yet redeem themselves through development of deep character. Thriller nemeses can be attractive in their characterization, yet repugnant in their deep character. Thrillers afford more freedom, in the design of central characters, than any other mode of fiction.

Multiple protagonists are used in thrillers where the guys we're rooting for are a team. They may not work together as a team – and often the friction generated between them compounds the conflict of the story – yet they represent the positive energies of the novel. Combat or wartime thrillers naturally use this device heavily, as do heist-stories.

Organized-crime stories can combine multiple protagonists too – think of the movie *Pulp Fiction*, where the protagonists are two footsoldier gangsters and a boxer fallen foul of their boss. The three-way split powers an exhilarating and action-packed thriller. The key to its success, as with most multiple-protagonist stories, are the zones where the three paths intersect.

Tempered by fire: heroes who 'arc'

Homicide cop Sonchai Jitpleecheep is, as we've seen, a hero in a state of constant flux, with many different roles to fulfil.

When he's not busting down the doors of Thai tradition to solve fiendishly challenging murders, he's playing envoy to his boss – in police matters, on gangster business, or often both at once. When he's not representing Colonel Vikorn's interests, Sonchai is obliged to his brothel-keeping mother's. All the while he's struggling, as a locked-and-loaded Buddhist monk, with the thorny questions of existence.

As if that wasn't enough, each novel in John Burdett's thriller series throws him a tough personal challenge. In the first, his 'soul-brother' is horribly killed in the opening pages, at the murder scene which drives the main plot. Through the personal subplot of the novel, narrated to complement the twists and turns of his homicide investigation, Sonchai must adjust to life alone on this mortal coil.

In another novel he meets his predestined soul mate, the woman the universe wants him to be with. She's a bar-girl hooker, the very last person a young cop should take for a wife. When Sonchai first meets her, and realizes their destiny together, things are even less auspicious – her last client, an American sex-tourist, has just been mutilated and murdered in her bed, a crime she freely confesses to.

Another Burdett thriller sees Sonchai reunited with his dead friend, when his first child is born. Sonchai's baby son is the reincarnation of his soul-brother's mischievous spirit, but terrible events lie ahead. Through powerful personal adversity, narrated in tandem with both the main homicide plot and subplots driven by his boss or mother, Sonchai undergoes powerful processes of personal change.

These processes are called *arcs of character*. The hero starts from an opening position – how they're squared with the world as it stands – and ends in a different place, educated for better or worse by the events of the plot. Life is a process of change, of adjusting to new challenges, so 'arcing' stories often tell very human stories. They're often concerned with changes in personal values or self-perception. They usually involve not a simple reversal in these personal issues but a more complex journey.

Arcs of change can be for good or bad. The wealthy man in *The Tortilla Curtain* arcs from being a model citizen to a homicidal paranoiac. The secret agent in *The Honourable Schoolboy* – the guy who jokes about his enemy's portrait – arcs from being his masters' dutiful instrument, to steering his own ship.

Thrillers which arc their hero use the events of the story to do so. The plot is not simply designed to narrate the face-off between protagonist and nemesis, but to excavate and test the hero's deep character.

Key idea

'Character-driven' is a term that's used often about fiction, usually wrongly. It doesn't mean that the principals in a story are attractive, intriguing people; that's their characterization, not their character. Deep character is the true fuel of 'character-driven' fiction, where gripping plots are designed to draw out and test true-character to its utmost, leading the protagonist – and sometimes the antagonist – through powerful arcs of change.

John Burdett's Bangkok thrillers are rare for having a series protagonist who arcs in each novel. Series tend to use non-arcing protagonists. Heroes like James Bond or Jack Reacher remain essentially unchanged by their adventures. They're a few days older and wiser, maybe, but essentially they're the same guy at the end of each novel as they were at the start. Series-fans generally know what they'll be getting when they sit down to read.

But some thrillers use a recurring protagonist to tell powerful stories of change. A series hero who arcs is Alex Cross, in James Patterson's thrillers – we'll examine Cross in detail in Chapter 7. Another protagonist who arcs is Clarice Starling, in the

'Hannibal Lecter' thrillers. The blockbusting movie, *The Silence Of The Lambs*, adapted from Thomas Harris' thriller, began by presenting her visually – Clarice jogging through woodlands, hair tied back in a ponytail, her sweats emblazoned with 'FBI' as if it was the name of a university. She's a sophomore, we surmise, a rookie Federal agent.

The Federal Bureau of Investigation is a fruitful institution for thriller writers to exploit. Cops are venal – two words will suffice here: Dunkin' Donuts – but Feds inhabit a higher plane. To the federal agent, the line between good guys and bad guys is clearly delineated. The good guys wear the FBI badge, end of story.

Thomas Harris used this idea to open his mega-selling novel. Agent Starling believes that she's on the side of the good guys. That the only people to learn from in life are lecturers, back at FBI Academy. Then she meets Dr Lecter.

He's a trained psychologist, a man as remarkable for his intelligence as the horror of his crimes. Clarice visits him, in a high-security jail, to garner clues about a serial killer on the loose.

It's a set-up that delivers a powerful *arc of change* for Clarice. Because, far from being a criminal man with a criminal mind – as Clarice has been led to believe all criminals are, by her tutors – Lecter comes across as an urbane and intelligent man, sophisticated and witty yet unflinching in the clarity of his insights.

Some of these insights affect Clarice deeply, and personally. Over the course of the novel, Lecter skilfully yet sternly demolishes Clarice's sense of who she is. He turns her from a greenhorn, wet behind the ears and believing in a fairytale world of good and bad, into a clear-eyed adult. He isolates the moments in her childhood when this fairytale view was fixed – the death of her father, a cop on active duty, and the moment soon afterward when she realized that lambs aren't reared to be fluffy playmates for little girls, but for meat – and helps her relinquish the legacy of these traumas forever.

In doing so, Lecter helps Clarice catch her killer. She does so as an adult, not as a rookie, finding the courage and resources to face down a monster single-handed. The thriller *arcs* her from an *opening position* of immaturity to a *closing position* of adult self-sufficiency. For Clarice, wishful thinking about 'criminal types' has been made obsolete. The line between good guys and bad guys has been blurred, permanently.

It's a story about moving on, psychologically, for the protagonist. It ends with Hannibal Lecter moving on physically, escaping jail and disappearing into a new identity. A versatile villain, and one of the most memorable in thriller history. In the next chapter we'll examine that crucial component of all thrillers – the mastermind, the boss of the bad guys, the antagonist. First let's recap the key concepts about heroes, to take forward into our study of the villain.

Focus points

All heroes need attributes to help them reach – and survive – the end of the line. The key to successful characterization isn't installing these attributes in your hero, but planting their seeds in 'backstory', so that the unfolding action can draw-out and develop these key attributes.

The contrast between surface and depth, between appearance and reality, makes principal characters come alive. It's the human condition – who among us doesn't believe that we are more than we appear to be?

If your hero is employed – a cop, a spy, a customs-agent – does their work limit the potential to push jeopardy to the end of the line? If so, the key to taking them 'off-leash' credibly is to make it a natural development – after all, the hero doesn't know that the end of the line is looming. Don't make them burn bridges just to get your story moving.

'Little guy' protagonists anchor vigorous human stories. Does your thriller need powerful identification with an intensely human situation? Is it about stepping up, and doing the right thing, whatever the consequences? Use a little-guy protagonist. But if your story needs a little-guy protagonist, yet necessary story events seem beyond their reach, consider a dual- or multiple-protagonist setup.

Many thriller protagonists don't 'arc', but those who do arc powerfully. Thrillers push the stakes as high as they can go – powerful change is usually required to meet the demands of the action.

The Thriller Villain

In this chapter you will learn:

▶ *How great thriller villains are designed and constructed*

▶ *What a villain needs to push the action to the end of the line*

▶ *The formula to build a story from the basic conflict between your hero and villain*

▶ *How to maximize your face-offs, from first skirmish to final showdown*

Hero and villain – the deadly embrace

Thriller villains make some of the most memorable characters in fiction. Their dastardly menace and chilling misdeeds are staples of popular culture. Think of the cat-stroking Bond villain Blofeld, or Hannibal the Cannibal, or the shark in Peter Benchley's serial killer thriller *Jaws*.

Blood-curdling, powerful adversaries. And they need to be, because if the conflict of a thriller is going to push the hero to the end of the line, then the forces of antagonism must be equal to the task. They must be powerful enough not only to trigger all-out combat, but to escalate it to the absolute end of the protagonist's personal line. This is the deadly embrace between villain and hero.

Hannibal Lecter is a powerful antagonist, and one of the most famous villains ever. There are few corners of the world where his chilling mannerisms aren't recognized if imitated. 'Shaken not stirred' may be one of the most quoted bits of dialogue there is, but Lecter's most bloodcurdling expression – that horrid gobbling noise he makes, after the line about fava beans and Chianti – is equally well known.

Ask anyone who Hannibal Lecter is, and they'll say he's the villain of *The Silence of the Lambs*. And they'll be right. But, to anyone who knows even the basics of the plot, there's a massive contradiction in that statement.

Hannibal the Cannibal may be a serial killer, but he's in prison for most of the story. He's already caught. The serial killer who drives the plot is another guy entirely – 'Buffalo Bill', who skins his victims.

It's Buffalo Bill who must be caught before he strikes again. Not Lecter. Buffalo Bill is the murderer on the loose. Lecter is already in prison. Yet he's the true villain. Why?

Let's look at him in a little more detail. Lecter is a serial killer who cannibalizes his victims. He eats them. This is the great evil that he's known for. A true end-of-the-line, if the line we're talking about is murder. Lecter doesn't just turn living people into dead meat, he cooks them up and washes them down with fine wine.

It's a big-screen, blockbusting kind of evil. But Clarice Starling, the heroine pitted against Lecter, does not personally fear his cannibalism. She's jittery on her first visit to the jail, certainly, but as soon as she gets talking with Lecter it fades.

So Lecter's big evil – cannibalism – is not an issue between the principal characters, as the story unfolds. Lecter doesn't desire to cook or otherwise eat Clarice Starling. And for her part, she's not trying to put the cannibal behind bars; he's already there.

Which isn't to say that Lecter's cannibalism isn't important. From the very start, it adds powerful *frisson* to scenes, like the very first meeting – where the reinforced glass between Clarice and Lecter, and the security drawer for passing items between them, are used to their utmost potential for chilling suspense. But cannibalism is not the central issue of the story. In plot terms, it's a sideshow.

It's an attribute of characterization, not of deep character. Lecter *looks* like a psycho, at first impression. He's a guy kept in maximum security for a reason. The other psychos in his jail block have bars to their cells, Lecter's has bomb-proof glass. A steel cage isn't safe enough, for this monster.

He looks like the craziest man possible when we first see him, in the depths of maximum security. But in the action that follows, where we get to judge him for ourselves, Lecter comes across as a supremely intelligent and insightful psychologist. He moves from crazy, in the author's presentation of his character, to the polar opposite – a brilliant psychologist, the guy who cures crazy.

The thriller villain – characterization versus deep character

It's a powerful reversal of expectation, a great twist on the opening positions of the principals. But that's who Lecter proves to be, as he dismantles the training academy confidence of a rookie Fed, and coaxes out her deepest horrors.

It's a powerful psychological catharsis, and the culmination of powerful conflict between Starling and the good doctor. In Thomas Harris' masterful presentation of his antagonist, Lecter transmutes from crazy man to mentor, from evil-doer to healer. A powerful twist, across the course of the novel. But it doesn't make Lecter any less the antagonist of the story.

Remember this

Just as thriller heroes need strong contrast between characterization and true character, so thriller villains need a powerful difference between who they appear to be and who they really are. It's these gaps — between what the reader is led to expect and what actually happens — that generate powerful reversals of expectation in a thriller. Powerful twists.

Let's look at those famous Bond villains again. What they appear to be, at first impression, are wack jobs. Island-owning crazies, with private armies and a burning desire for world domination. Megalomaniac nuts.

That's what they look like, in the early skirmishes of Bond thrillers. But as the conflict escalates, we see a more chilling side to these delusional tycoons. Remember the scene in Ian Fleming's classic thriller *Goldfinger*, with Bond strapped to a table, a steel-cutting laser advancing between his legs? In the first chapter, Bond catches Goldfinger cheating at cards. Bond challenges the tycoon to a game of golf, only to find he cheats at that too. We get the picture. This is a billionaire with a pathological need to win at everything he does, however petty.

The card game and the golf match cut Goldfinger down to size for us. He's a childish cheat. The sport of the game is nothing to him – like a self-centred brat, all he cares about is victory. Once we've seen this villain in action, we feel confident that Bond will either put this guy in jail or take him out entirely. We expect Bond to win.

But it's a fast ride from that confident opening position to utter defeat – the laser advancing between Bond's legs, and Goldfinger's chilling one-liner. The opening position of the novel is turned on its head. It's another powerful reversal of expectation, created again by working the opposition between *characterization* and *deep character* in the presentation of the antagonist.

The first few chapters of *Goldfinger* suggest to us that Bond will win this tussle hands down. The villain is presented as a privileged brat who thinks the rules don't apply to rich guys. Time for a major wake-up call. And James Bond, we know, is the man to deliver it.

But before we know it 007 is strapped to a steel table, and about to die horribly at Goldfinger's hands. His desperate attempt to buy a few seconds, before the laser slices him in two – 'Do you expect me to talk?' – falls on flinty ground. Goldfinger, it turns out, is rich for a reason.

He's an operator. A strategist, ruthless in his single-mindedness. When the seconds are counting down for Bond, with the laser advancing rapidly towards his testicles, Goldfinger isn't interested in talking. He's interested in winning. And in this game it appears that he already has.

The brinksmanship that Bond desperately tries to initiate, in the quote above, is of as little interest to Goldfinger as the game of cards, or the golf-match. All he cares about is winning.

And for now, victory means James Bond cut in two by a laser, and the two halves dumped outside M's office. If Goldfinger can dispatch the elite top-gun of enforcement so shockingly, then enforcement is on the defensive from that point on. Goldfinger can carry out his threats from a confident, attacking position. People who start with 'the upper hand' tend to win.

So this villain represents powerful forces of antagonism. His characterization, as a childish cheat, is developed by the events of the story, drawing out his true character – a ruthless, unstoppable operator. The cheating spoilt brat proves to be the most fearsome adversary Bond has encountered. The laser is certainly the nearest Bond gets to absolute defeat.

Villains: appearance and reality

The classic thriller nemesis Goldfinger shows us that the contrast between first impressions and actuality, so vital to the presentation of the hero, is equally important in the construction of the villain.

In Hannibal Lecter, we see the same sharp contrast between appearance and actuality defined by the events of the story. Lecter 'appears' to be a psycho, a frenzied killer for whom killing is only half the fun. He uses gourmet skills to *sauté* his victims' organs, then savours them with fine wine. As serial killers go, it doesn't get more way-out than that.

But Lecter's murderousness is not what the plot turns upon. Agent Starling is trying to catch a grisly serial killer, but it's not Lecter. He's already caught. He is, nonetheless, the villain of the thriller. The antagonist.

Yet he's not a culprit, to be tracked and unmasked. That's the role of the *perpetrator* in the plot – the crazed serial killer whom Clarice must catch before he kills again. This is a seriously nasty guy. 'Buffalo Bill' abducts young women, keeps them in a hole in the ground, starves them, makes them do weird things with lotion. Then he kills them and skins them. A horribly insane criminal, but he's not the villain. He's the perpetrator in the story. Lecter is the antagonist.

This is where Harris' construction of his villain gets truly fiendish. *Lecter doesn't do anything villainous in the story.* On the contrary, he helps Agent Starling catch her serial killer.

Lecter does so by truly giving of himself. Exercising his renowned psychoanalytic skills to help Starling win through. In *The Silence of the Lambs*, Doctor Hannibal Lecter makes a positive contribution to society. Yet still, he's the antagonist of the thriller.

Towards the story's end, Lecter kills a few guards when he escapes from jail, plus a corrupt prison governor, it's true. But these murders aren't villainous. On the contrary, they're killings we don't entirely disapprove of. The guards whom Lecter kills are sadistic bullies, and the governor – someone we've seen crudely trying to strong-arm Clarice – is a scumbag. The manner in which Lecter dispatches them is not a nice way to die, certainly, but most of us would agree that the world of the story is not worse off without these people.

So even the horrific murders Lecter commits in the novel aren't villainous. Yet ask anyone who Hannibal Lecter is, and they'll say he's the villain of *The Silence of the Lambs*. And they'll be right.

The novel's plot is driven by the search for a serial killer, a guy who must be caught before he kills again, but Lecter represents the forces of antagonism in the novel. The meaningful conflict of this powerful thriller is not between Starling and Buffalo Bill, but Starling and Lecter. So Lecter is one of the greatest antagonists in fictional history, yet he does nothing we condemn in the action of this novel.

The antagonist and the end of the line

Lecter is the villain of Thomas Harris' thriller because he embodies the forces which push Clarice Starling to the end of her personal line.

That's what thrillers do. The goal is to push conflict – and therefore jeopardy – as far as it can desperately go. Catching culprits is the objective of crime stories, mysteries and whodunnits. The solution to the mystery, the unmasking of the perpetrator, is the big pay-off of a crime novel. Thrillers go deeper.

Key idea

In thrillers, our focus is on the end of the line. Crimes may be solved in the process, but pushing the conflict to its utmost is the primary concern.

In *The Silence of the Lambs*, Lecter is the character who takes things to the end of the line. But he's long gone before the climax of the novel – a scene, nonetheless, of heartstopping suspense. The protagonist, Agent Starling, is a lone cop in a cavernous lair, stalking a horrific serial killer who's skulking somewhere in the shadows. Lecter knows this killer, from way back. From the moment Starling revealed her objective, he knew it was always going to come to this.

From the very start. And he knew that the rookie Clarice Starling wouldn't have lasted a minute in this kind of showdown. When Lecter meets Starling, she's a greenhorn who believes that catching killers is a matter of profiling – not groping in the dark of enemy territory with a drawn weapon.

So Lecter decides to actually help this rookie agent, after Starling shows him her mettle through the course of their first skirmish. He uses his professional skills to prepare her for the task of taking down Buffalo Bill.

Lecter knows the kind of mental fortitude that will be required to see the job through. And he sees potential in Clarice Starling, at their first encounter, but also that she's nowhere near ready for the job she's taken on.

So Lecter goes to work, in his role as world-renowned psychologist. He frees Starling of 'black-and-white thinking' – the kind of false perception which can occlude a cop's vision, with fatal consequences. It's a tough job for Lecter, because in Starling this mindset was ingrained by childhood traumas. The violent death of her father on police duty, and the screaming of lambs in a slaughterhouse soon after.

Lecter leads Starling through a psychotherapeutic process, designed to help the young woman anchor herself in the adult world. He helps Starling move on from the traumas – get closure, by talking out the buried horrors of her childhood – so she won't freeze like a terrified child when the showdown with Buffalo Bill comes.

Try it now

Think of a dark secret. Something awful that happens, which people have to move on from in life. Write it down and put it in your pocket.

Now take your notebook to a crowded train platform, or a vantage point on a busy street. Pick the first person your eye settles on out of the crowd. Without staring, look at them as closely as you can. Take in everything that there is to take in about them. Now take your dark secret from your pocket, and put it into this person's life.

How did it affect them? How did they cope? How did their demeanour and behaviour adapt to do so? What new skills did they have to learn? Were 'negative' actions necessary to move on – e.g. cutting people out of their lives – as well as positive ones? How did these affect their everyday routines? Break it down, examining your thinking at each step, and keep your notes for reference – this is the process of figuring out deep character versus surface characterization. In practising this skill, you will soon begin identifying core values in the contrast between the two.

In *The Silence of the Lambs*, Lecter's brutally efficient psychotherapy has the desired effect. In the final face-off of the story, Starling must enter the killer's lair alone, to save his latest victim. She doesn't freeze up, or jump out of her skin at the first noise and start blazing away with her weapon. She plays a heart-in-mouth game of cat and mouse – or vice versa – and sees it through.

Catching the killer is the final face-off of the novel, but the scenes between Starling and Lecter are its real conflict. A battle between a victim of childhood trauma, and the defences she's constructed because of it, and a psychologist who understands that those defences have to go if the trauma is to be relinquished.

This is Starling's personal end-of-the-line. This is the terrain she must fight, if she's to win the war. Catching the perpetrator is the endgame of the exercise, and indeed it follows: Starling catches the killer before he kills again. But only after the epic battle between Dr Lecter and Agent Starling's psychological defences. A battle which Starling must lose, in order to win.

This antagonist, then, does a lot of good in the novel. He helps Clarice on a professional level, and a personal one. He kills a few scumbags and escapes, but when Clarice receives a letter from him in the novel's closing scene, we are delighted. For her, as well as ourselves, in getting one last chance to hear from the good doctor. We feel a strong positive emotion for Clarice as she reads the handwritten lines. It's a moving scene, and a fine conclusion to a brilliant thriller.

Using the antagonist to build plot

Hannibal Lecter shows us that the antagonist in the novel – the protagonist's true opposite number – drives its central conflict.

In a thriller, this conflict can override even the most perilous pursuit of a perpetrator. In *The Silence of the Lambs* the capture of Buffalo Bill is consequent on the conflict between Lecter and Starling.

The conflict of the plot interrogates the central human value of the story: *loyalty*. At the start, Clarice is loyal to the FBI, and to trendy theories of criminology. She's embedded with the good guys, and the rest of the world lies beyond the barbed-wire fence. Her loyalty to her badge is absolute.

Then she meets Lecter. His insights split that loyalty. The FBI's golden girl is now taking professional advice from a maximum-security convict. Worse, she's letting him take her psyche to pieces. Lecter's magnetic influence cuts Clarice's seemingly impregnable position in two. The story moves her from a position of absolute loyalty, to one of *split allegiance*.

By the closing scene she's gone all the way – from loyalty to the FBI to *betrayal*. She receives a handwritten note from Lecter, a fugitive killer, someone who murdered prison staff to escape. But Starling doesn't hand the letter to her bosses. She reads it, relishing every word, then tucks it away.

The rookie who began the novel would've gone all-out on the letter, getting it analysed, looking for telltale pollen or dust that might give away Lecter's location. The mature Clarice smiles and gets on with her day. The FBI team hunting Lecter will not be seeing this piece of evidence, we realize. Clarice has moved all the way from loyalty to the FBI to loyalty to Lecter. In the story's powerful closing scene she betrays the Bureau, the institution that she belonged to, body and soul, at the start.

So the progression that the antagonist forces in Starling's core values breaks down like this:

```
┌─────────────────┐
│    LOYALTY      │
│   (opening)     │
└─────────────────┘
         │
         ▼
┌─────────────────┐
│ SPLIT ALLEGIANCE│
│   (conflict)    │
└─────────────────┘
         │
         ▼
┌─────────────────┐
│    BETRAYAL     │
│    (ending)     │
└─────────────────┘
```

It moves from the opening position of loyalty to its *middle-ground* position, split allegiance. The novel's pay-off confirms that the *opposite* value to loyalty, betrayal, has been reached.

But this isn't a straight betrayal, it's a position we applaud in Clarice. Turning Lecter's letter over to her bosses would be churlish at this point, even childish. She's grown up, become a balanced adult, not an FBI robot.

This 'positive' betrayal is the conclusion to a powerful novel about human change. Starlings are birds famous for flocking together, in vast numbers. In northern climes, their sunset swarms fill the sky. By the end of Harris' powerful thriller, this Starling has learned to fly alone.

THE ANTAGONIST AND THE ULTIMATE BATTLE

But this final-scene 'betrayal' is not the end of the line for Clarice. In thrillers, the end of the line comes before the end of the book. It's by going to the end of the line that a final battle can be waged and a resolution reached. The resolution, in itself, is rarely the end of the line.

To see how, let's look again at that value of *loyalty*, which the forces of antagonism develop in Starling. *Loyalty* has an obvious opposite – *betrayal*. And there's a middle ground between *loyalty* and *betrayal* – *split allegiance*. We've identified these three positions in our analysis of the progress of this story.

But most human values have not only an opposite position, and a middle ground between the two, but an end-of-the-line position too. *Loyalty* is no exception. The middle ground is *split allegiance*, the opposite value is *betrayal*. The end-of-the-line is *self-betrayal*.

🔑 Key idea

The end of the line is the opposite value pushed as far as it can go. Betrayal is bad, but self-betrayal is a highway to hell. Someone who betrays others is on dangerous ground. Those who betray themselves are finished. Self-betrayal is the end of the line, when loyalty is the opening value.

The genius of *The Silence of the Lambs* is not just to build the progression so tightly, but to reverse the conventional polarity on all these values. Starling's *loyalty* is negative in this story – it's giving her a fairytale view of the world, a rookie's false confidence. As she falls under Lecter's spell, her consequent *split allegiance* becomes a positive development, even as we fear for her.

We know that it's playing with fire, for a Fed to make herself vulnerable to a master criminal. But there are positive outcomes from the initial interviews with Lecter. Starling gains insights into the murders which triggered the plot, and begins her development into a fully formed adult, by splitting her allegiance. It's a positive act for Clarice.

Her *self-betrayal* comes when she talks through the traumas of her childhood with Dr Lecter. It's a self-betrayal because the energies of her life have been expended on burying these traumas deep. They're the reason she's an FBI automaton, with no life of her own, at the start of the action.

To move on, and become a rounded adult, Starling must expose the psychological defences that surviving her traumatic childhood depended upon. Not only must she expose them, she must allow a skilled therapist to dismantle them. These defences may have helped her survive horrible experiences as a kid, but in adult life they're holding her back.

So the complete progression on the core-value in Starling's story runs like this:

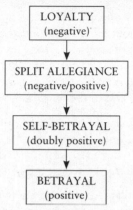

LOYALTY
(negative)

↓

SPLIT ALLEGIANCE
(negative/positive)

↓

SELF-BETRAYAL
(doubly positive)

↓

BETRAYAL
(positive)

The end of the line – the most powerful variation on the core value of 'loyalty', self-betrayal – comes before the end of the progression. It sets up the ending, and makes it possible.

Conflict: the four-part progression

Let's try the process with another example. *Justice* is the central value of many thrillers. A crime has been committed, the world has been changed. To set things right, the hero must go to the end of the line. Here's how the four-part progression plays out with the value of *justice*:

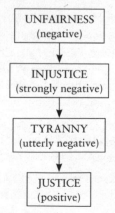

UNFAIRNESS
(negative)

↓

INJUSTICE
(strongly negative)

↓

TYRANNY
(utterly negative)

↓

JUSTICE
(positive)

It's a straightforward process, escalating wrongdoing to a final showdown and a positive outcome.

Goldfinger uses this sequence. The novel opens with Bond catching the eponymous villain cheating at cards, then at golf. It's not an ideal state of affairs, if people at the top of the pile behave this way, but life goes on. The value of *unfairness* is explored in the opening of the story, but it's only a guy cheating at games. It's not the end of the world.

The progression escalates to *injustice* as Goldfinger's big crime comes into focus. No mixed charge on this one. The progression moves from relatively inconsequential *unfairness* to all-out wrong. Injustice is charged unequivocally negative.

Bond takes on the villain, and loses. Soon he's strapped to a steel table in Goldfinger's lair, facing his own execution. Bond has gone deeper into Goldfinger's world, from catching him cheating to trying to take him down. But Goldfinger has proved a stronger adversary than anticipated. Now Bond is subject to this wealthy wacko's *tyranny*, as he reaches the end of the line.

In this classic thriller, the end of the line is literal. The road that Bond sets out on, when he begins to pursue Goldfinger, ends in the villain's lair. The end of the line is Bond as a helpless prisoner, desperately trying to bargain for his life – 'Do you expect me to talk?'

Bond survives, of course, and wins the day. But he has to go to the end of the line to do so. He has to infiltrate Goldfinger's lair and risk a horrible death – inches away, quite literally, in the laser-scene – to attack this villain's fatal flaw. The progression on the value of 'justice' dictates the action of the novel.

Try it now

Consider the core value *love*. The middle ground and opposite positions are obvious. What is at the end of the line, when *love* is the core value?

If you've only come up with one answer, think again. There are two possible end-of-the-line positions here, both of which negate the core value

Progressing the core value is how thriller authors create story. When planning a novel, we decide on the value we want to interrogate. We work out the possible progressions on that value. In the case of *justice*, or *loyalty* these are:

▶ the *middle-ground* position – justice is *unfairness*, loyalty is *split-allegiance*

▶ the *opposite* position – justice is *injustice*, loyalty is *betrayal*

▶ the *ultimate* position – justice is *tyranny*, loyalty is *self-betrayal*.

Breaking it down gives us four positions on the value. *Justice*, *unfairness*, *injustice* and *tyranny*. Or *loyalty*, *split-allegiance*, *betrayal* and *self-betrayal*. And with four positions to peg our planning to, the substance of story immediately begins to emerge.

Remember this

Rethinking the 'obvious' charges on values – e.g. making loyalty negative, as with Starling's robot-like loyalty to the FBI – can open up yet more opportunities for a compelling story. Loyalty charged negative opens up intriguing possibilities for the end-of-the-line position – as in Starling's story, where self-betrayal becomes powerfully positive, creating surprise and depth in Thomas Harris' classic thriller.

CORE-VALUE PROGRESSIONS: DETAILED EXAMPLES

The four-position breakdown works with any human value. *Truth* is the value which drives political and ethical thrillers. Its middle-ground position is 'white lies' – harmless untruths. Its opposite position is outright deception. The end of the line with this value is *self-deception*; hell in a handcart, in anyone's book.

Courage is often the core-value in 'little-guy' protagonist thrillers, where a civilian must step up and fight to the end of the line. The middle-ground position on this value is *fear*; this may be where a civilian hero is at the start of a story, living in fear. The opposite value is *cowardice*, which the protagonist must overcome if they're to step up and overcome the forces of antagonism. But if fear overcomes them at the crucial moment, they may seek to lose, backing-off whilst trying to save face. This is the end of the line – *cowardice* masquerading as *courage*.

Success is a fundamental core value. Thrillers may begin or end with it, or do both. Its middle ground is compromise, which may equally be an opening position. The opposite value to success is, obviously, *failure*. Again this may be an opening position, as may the end of the line – *selling-out*. As the saying goes, everyone has their price when the chips are truly down.

Try it now

Think of one of the thrillers you've most enjoyed. What's its central idea? Which human value is tested by the characters and events of the story? Can you identify an opening position? How has that value changed by the end of the thriller? What caused the change?

Identify the steps in between the opening and closing positions, and you will soon be able to isolate the middle ground, opposite and ultimate positions on a value, and the positive or negative charges applied. Do this for as many good thrillers as you can, and write the four-part positions under each other on a large sheet of paper, with their positive or negative charges. Use this sheet as a map of the realm of the possible when you return to your own thriller.

Wealth is a core value which naturally fuels many thrillers. Its middle-ground position is where most people are – *surviving*, with money to meet life's needs but not much more. The opposite position to *wealth* is *poverty*. It means not having enough money to live, and people die from poverty every second, but it's not the end of the line in story terms.

The ultimate position on this value mixes poverty with wealth. Someone who's rich, but thinks like they're poor. Like every minute of every day has to be spent in the pursuit of yet more money.

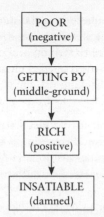

POOR
(negative)

↓

GETTING BY
(middle-ground)

↓

RICH
(positive)

↓

INSATIABLE
(damned)

The fourth, final progression on the core value is the end of the line. It's the point beyond which the story cannot go. Working the value of *wealth* has always been fruitful ground for fiction – a villainous archetype is the rich guy who can't be satisfied, from King Midas to Bond's nemeses to Gordon 'Greed Is Good' Gekko. Storytellers have worked the four-part progression on this value since money was invented.

The end of the line and the final showdown

The end-of-the-line scene is one of the most visceral and powerful in a thriller. But it's rarely the end of the line in story terms.

In *Tinker Tailor Soldier Spy*, the end-of-the-line scene comes when George Smiley arrests his closest colleague, his best friend and his wife's lover, for treason. But the antagonist, Karla, remains to be fought. The 'screaming of the lambs' scene is Clarice Starling's personal end of the line, yet once it's over she still has to locate and take down Buffalo Bill.

Key idea

The end of the line represents the final big turning-point of the story. It's where the protagonist and the forces of antagonism fight the decisive battle. The final battle is another matter entirely, and may not involve the antagonist at all.

Lecter is long gone, escaped from jail and vanished, by the time Clarice stalks her serial killer in the shadows of his lair. The end-of-the-line scene pushes the stakes to their utmost, and slingshots the action forward into its ultimate sequence.

Remember this

The final battle often comes after the end of the line in stories that maximize to the utmost their potential for power. The two events can be constructed to turbo-charge the last sequence, with the end-of-the-line scenes fuelling the explosiveness of the final showdown.

The end of the line is where the forces of antagonism bring the story. It's what these forces are designed to do by thriller authors, quite deliberately; the antagonist is carefully designed to make the protagonist face their personal ultimate test of character. Great villains, like great heroes, don't come from 'eureka' moments of lightning-bolt inspiration but from working the craft of story.

Now it's time to explore the first crucial element in any thriller – the opening sequence. We'll study in depth how opening sequences are built to get thrillers accelerating fast, explore which kind of opening is right for your novel, and isolate each of the objectives an opening-sequence needs to nail down, to avoid the pitfalls that these critical scenes encounter. First let's recap the key insights about villains to take forward.

Focus points

A thriller villain doesn't have to be dastardly or 'villainous' to fuel a successful thriller – but they must have the power to push the conflict all the way to the protagonist's personal end of the line.

Just as the hero must have a rich contrast between initial characterization and deep character, so must the villain, if the conflict they provoke is to be explosive enough to attain the end of the line.

The 'end of the line' is the ultimate position on the story's core value. It can be doubly negative or doubly positive, but never somewhere in between. It must represent the most extreme variation on the core value that the possibilities of human life can produce.

Reversing conventional charges on values – making 'loyalty' negative, for example – can produce original, groundbreaking stories whilst setting up a positively charged ending.

The end of the line and the final showdown need not be the same scene. Splitting them – mid-act climax and act climax, for example – can turbo-charge the final movement of a thriller, fuelling the explosiveness of the ending.

The Trigger

In this chapter you will learn:

▶ *What a thriller needs to get moving on the page*

▶ *Where to open your thriller story*

▶ *Whether to use a high-impact trigger or a slow-burn to detonation*

▶ *What a trigger must do to maximize impact and effect*

Thriller opening sequences

The first pages of any novel need to do many things at once.

Firstly, they have to answer the famous storytelling questions: *when, where, who* and *what*. Long ago, in a kingdom far away, a knight rode out to rescue a princess.

It's a convention we're familiar with from early childhood. So familiar that, sometimes, an opening will leave us to fill in the blanks. The first line of George Orwell's dystopian thriller *Nineteen Eighty-Four* runs:

> It was a bright cold day in April, and the clocks were striking thirteen.

A complex *when* situation is established with a single word – that thirteen o'clock. This, we understand, is the future.

But it's confirming what we already know. Published in 1949, Orwell's title delivers that fact. So his great hook line isn't just telling us it's the future, it's telling us what kind of future it is: *a bright cold day*. It's a future where the weather still makes a difference. Not an insulated, high-tech society, but a world where people still feel the cold, and appreciate a little sunshine – and so it proves, in Winston Smith's world of dank tenements, threadbare clothing and scant food.

This dystopian future is fleshed out as the story unfolds, but its opening sentence establishes both the world of the novel, its big surprise, and its visionary central message – the future may not be a better place, if we continue on our current path.

All opening sequences need to set up who we're following in the story, and what they do in their lives. What kind of world they live in and when. Who the other people in that world are, and its power dynamics (put simply, its pecking order).

The latter is especially important, because the first friction of the novel's action may derive from the opening's power-setup. Friction between a cop and a boss-cop, or a cop and a criminal. Friction between a worker and a supervisor, or a secret agent and their opposite number. The kind of friction that propels a protagonist into a plot, and sets them on their quest.

The first pages of a thriller must also set-up the trigger incident, or deliver it straightaway. In doing so it must present an immediate situation that intrigues us, and makes us want to read on.

In publishing terms, the opening pages are crucial. Agents and editors crack open hundreds of manuscripts a year. If the first pages of a story don't grab them, they must move on to the next. Ditto sales reps and bookstore buyers. The nature of the job means they have to be able to tell whether a novel's got what it takes from its opening pages alone.

Similarly, people shopping for a novel do two things when they pick up a book. They read what's on the cover, and they flip to the opening page. If the latter doesn't intrigue them, they replace the book and reach for another.

Thrillers aim to set pulses racing from the very first page. They do this by establishing the world of the novel, using storytelling skills to make us feel it in our guts, and often pitching us straight into heart-stopping action.

Hitting the ground running: high-impact openings

In Robert Ludlum's *The Bourne Identity*, the hero is found floating in open ocean by a fishing boat. He's unconscious with gunshot wounds. When a fisherman checks him over, there seems to be a small capsule implanted beneath the skin of his back. When the hero wakes up, he has no idea who he is or how he came to be in the water.

It's an extraordinary situation, anchored in the real world by all the detail of a creaking fishing boat at sea. An intriguing set-up is delivered powerfully and swiftly, and the story is off to a whiplash start.

In Emlyn Rees' recent thriller *Hunted*, the opening predicament is just as immediate. The hero wakes up to find himself in a strange hotel room with a dead man on the floor. The gun that killed him is in the hero's hands. He has no idea who the dead guy is, or if there are friends searching for him – or cops. He's in the middle of a city with police CCTV scanning every inch of every street, he has no cash or cards, and he's wearing bright red clothes. Game on, for a breakneck thrill-ride.

Try it now

Hit-the-ground-running sequences generate the opening action. For example, a guy wakes up with a sore head, a little fuzzy on exactly what happened before he passed out. For many writers, this is a not-unknown Sunday morning scenario. Fruitful complications could be:

✳ This isn't home, but a strange hotel room.

✳ There's a guy on the floor shot through the forehead.

✳ There's a used gun in the protagonist's hand.

Immediately, mystery drives the story forward, powered by immediate jeopardy. Try to inject mystery and jeopardy into these similar 'where am I' examples:

✳ on a highway hard shoulder carrying a sack

✳ in a fishing port wearing unsuitable clothes

✳ covered in mud in an airport.

Play with each scenario as if it's an opening sequence featuring a hero. Now make the central character in this sequence the villain of a story. What changes and how?

Without a hero: explosive set-ups for the protagonist

Openings which hit the ground running don't have to start with the hero. In Frederick Forsyth's *The Day of the Jackal* the action opens with a French army officer facing a firing-squad. After a few sharp paragraphs he is executed, for his part in a plot to assassinate the French president.

It's a tense, compelling opening scene. It answers the *when*, *where* and *what* of the novel. But the *who* of the story is thrown wide open. Up until the very last moment – until the firing-squad complete their assignment – we expect the officer to be saved by a last-minute reprieve, or in a guns-blazing rescue. But what happens instead is that the soldiers ready their weapons, and fire. The logical course of events is turned into a big surprise by the author. The storytelling convention – that the hero of the story will be the first character we see in a tough situation – is used to build suspense, right up to the second the bullets rip into flesh.

This is a powerful reversal of carefully led expectation. We thought we'd checked-off the big *who* box of our story-opening questions, and now the guy's dead.

Our next expectation – driven again by our familiarity with the conventions of storytelling – is this: well, the guy's dead, but maybe he's the hero after all. Maybe the story will go back in time now, and tell us how he wound up facing a firing squad.

Forsyth toys with us a little more here, because the story does indeed flash back at this point. But only briefly. Again there's a big reversal of our convention-led expectation, because this isn't a novel about the executed officer. The execution is the trigger to Forsyth's story – because, having tried and failed with their *coup d'état*, now the surviving plotters must search for a new assassin, beyond their own ranks this time. They find the eponymous Jackal, and Forsyth's classic novel narrates his lethal assignment, drawing us into the shadowy world of the professional hitman.

Slow-burn fuses: escalating openings

Many thrillers choose to hit the ground running. Their openings are high-impact, getting the adrenalin pumping and aiming to keep it there. Authors who want their thrillers to use every opportunity for edge-of-seat action take full advantage of an opening's possibilities to grab us by the guts.

But other kinds of thrillers take their time. Or seem to. In Chapter 3, we saw how the George Smiley novels broke the rules about heroes and villains to tell powerful, authentic stories. Their subject couldn't have been more serious at the time – the nuclear face-off between the Western powers and the Soviets. But despite these novels' power and urgent topical heft, the opening sequences they deploy aren't explosive in their ignition.

More a slow burn to detonation. Because in the opening scenes of each 'Karla' thriller, the story aims the zoom lens far from both hero and nemesis, delivering richly involving scene sequences full of the detail of everyday life, while the fuse burns slowly but inexorably off-stage.

Tinker Tailor Soldier Spy opens with a new teacher arriving at a provincial boys' school. He's an outdoorsy type who has a recent, troublesome injury in his back. The kids hero-worship their new teacher. He's a nice guy, who makes a point of befriending the bullied boys and taking their tormentors down a peg.

One of the kids is flummoxed, then, when he spots the new teacher doing strange things with the mail. Like he's trying to conceal his identity. Later, he sees him changing a homemade dressing on what appears to be a bullet wound in his shoulder. Then, after a stranger has come looking for the new teacher, the boy sees him digging up a cached revolver.

An engaging, richly textured piece of storytelling, but it doesn't build to the trigger for the story's action – it *is* the trigger. The new teacher turns out to be new to teaching indeed. He's a spy, shot in the back during a recent behind-the-lines operation. It's his betrayal that proves to Smiley there's a double agent at work amongst his colleagues.

The Honourable Schoolboy, the second novel in the trilogy, kicks off with a similarly rich sequence, of expat journalists in typhoon-bound Hong Kong, uncovering a strange story. This yarn is just set-up; the shocking truth the newshounds discover – Western intelligence is in retreat, with top-secret spy-stations boarded-up and for sale – is the state of the game for Smiley as the second book of the series begins. The trigger for this thriller follows swiftly, when Smiley's team unearth the first hint of their enemy's fatal flaw.

The trilogy's final showdown, *Smiley's People*, opens with a finely-told tale of an elderly Parisian widow menaced by a KGB thug. This set-up, as with the first book, contains the trigger – the widow writes a letter to an old underground contact, which ends up in Smiley's hands. Unlike action thrillers, which use explosive opening sequences to prove the hero's mettle right at the very start, John le Carré's acclaimed 'Karla' novels deploy rich, involving set-ups before the central characters take the stage, but the fuse is lit nonetheless.

Where to start? Positioning the opening sequence

We've explored a couple of novelists' maxims already – 'Less is more' and 'Show don't tell'. They're useful rules to follow. If you find yourself telling a reader what's going on, instead of showing them, then you're breaking faith with the reader; you promised them a story. Similarly, if you find yourself using too many words to flesh something out, and the pace starts to stall, then another approach is needed. 'Less is more' and 'show don't tell' are tried and tested maxims that all novelists should adhere to.

The storyteller's maxim governing where to begin and end a story – where in the chain of events of your plot to put page one and the closing scene – is this: 'Get in late, get out early'.

Key idea

'Get in late' sounds like a recipe for working hard and playing hard, but what it means to a storyteller looking to place their opening scene is simple. For best effect, begin the story as late in the chain of cause-and-effect which triggers the action as you possibly can.

The Silence of the Lambs doesn't open with the first of the serial slayings which drive the plot. It begins after several murders, when conventional efforts to catch the killer have failed. Lesser novelists might have focused on the horrors of the first murders, the desperation amongst Feds as the mutilated corpses of women keep appearing. Lots of opportunities for gore and tension there; but such a scene sequence would have been a series of foregone conclusions – we know that exotically characterized serial killers don't get caught in the first chapters of a thriller. So Thomas Harris doesn't start with the first murder. He puts his opening where it matters most – when the killer-catching stakes are ratcheted up, already, as far as they'll go. Harris starts the action as late in the chain of cause-and-effect as possible.

Tinker Tailor Soldier Spy doesn't start with the incident which proves there's a double agent at work. It starts with the aftermath of that incident. A spy with a bullet in his back, trying to pass himself off as a back-country schoolmaster while the dust settles. Again, the stakes are cranked to near breaking-point before the action begins.

Similarly, William Golding's literary thriller *Lord of the Flies* doesn't open with the plane crash which strands the boys on the island. It begins with a British schoolboy scrambling over rocks beside a tropical lagoon. The plane crash, with all its potential for white-knuckle immediacy, has already happened. We don't see it.

Golding's choice here greatly amplifies the potential for surprise and intrigue. Showing the plane crash would have given him a life-or-death opening scene, no doubt, but the big question – *how can these boys survive on a desert island?* – would still be the central driver. So Golding began his classic novel not by posing the big question, but by answering it.

He put the plane crash in the backstory, and opened instead with its aftermath. A plane crash is, after all, an arbitrary life-or-death situation. No one can do much to ensure their survival when a plane is in a fatal tailspin. But for the survivors, washed up on a tropical island like Robinson Crusoe or Tom Hanks in *Castaway*, their fate is in their own hands.

Most budding writers would have gone for the plane crash here. The chance for a big explosive scene to open would, for many, be hard to pass up. But in practice this approach would play out poorly, because stories which start by describing the passengers on a plane, and move swiftly on to the plane hitting turbulence, hold few surprises.

So Golding passed up the chance to narrate that particular life-or-death situation. Instead he started his story with the *next* life-or-death situation that crash survivors must face – how to stave off death until they're rescued. The genius of this opening is that Golding makes a grave life-or-death situation look like its polar opposite – a kid scrambling over seaside rocks in bright sunlight.

Swiftly we realize that this is not the scene we think it is, and the horror of the situation builds powerfully.

By *getting in late* to his story, Golding gave his readers a truly dramatic opening, rich with intrigue, and full of opportunities to set-up friction and conflict between the survivors. *Get out early* is the second part of the rule. It means: *Exit the scene as soon as you can.*

Remember this

One of the most common pitfalls I see in thriller manuscripts is when the action goes on for longer than it should, at both ends of a scene. Both exit and entry point must be calibrated for maximum power and impact, not permitted to meander and dilute these.

The closed circle – endings in beginnings

Remember Clarice Starling's four-part progression on her core value? It began with loyalty charged negatively and ended with a positive charge. It moved from an opening position on the story's core value to an opposite position at the close. So the ending of that twist-filled novel, despite whiplash reversals throughout, is set up by the opening.

A trigger should project the showdown. In *Jaws* a shark kills a swimmer off a tourist beach, and the police-chief finds the remains. In Elmore Leonard's *Out of Sight* a bank-robber escapes from jail. In *The Silence of the Lambs* a Fed seeks help to catch a killer. The endings are projected by the beginnings.

Because, in thrillers, we're working with tight logic. A story that begins by exploring an opening value will end with the logical closing value. The pattern of *core value* and *middle ground/ opposing/end of the line* direct the plot into a tight, closed loop. Part of a reader's pleasure, in the opening of a thriller, is second-guessing how this is going to end. The author's job is to intrigue and surprise a reader.

Remember this

An opening scene that does nothing beyond establishing what a tough guy the hero is, or what a sinister son-of-a-gun the villain, does not do its job. It's only checking one box, when a thriller requires several things at once from its opening, if it's to power-up to full potential. Chief among these is *meaningful* impact.

So a thriller writer must put a lot of thought into the opening scene. One of the most frequent reasons for a thriller to be rejected by publishers is because the opening is weak. Not *weak* as in nothing happens – usually these thrillers have explosive openings full of gunfire and mortal pursuit – but weak because they're empty noise.

Try it now

Pick four situations which might open a thriller. If you're stuck, try these: someone leaving a relationship; someone leaving a burning building; someone about to be pushed out of their job; someone about to be pushed out of a window.

Sketch out a thriller opening for each of your four situations. Concentrate on intrigue and meaningful impact. Someone who smells smoke, follows it to a blaze in a stairwell, and has to jump from a window to escape has little intrigue and no meaningful impact. Place your crises within human situations; imagine your openings are intended for a publisher to read, someone who must feel compelled to read on from the first lines. Plan them, then boil down your planning – is each of your decisions the most efficient way to deliver intrigue and impact? Now write a quick draft of each of your openings, then boil down the writing. Get it tight, and burning clean.

When you're satisfied, examine the scenes you've written. Isolate the opening value you've used in each case. For example, with someone leaving a burning building, you may have concentrated on a sense of loss. Or perhaps a sense of relief, in having all the baggage of a burdensome life incinerated.

Now find the closing position of each of your opening values. Take a fresh sheet, and sketch the four endings that are implied by your openings.

A high-impact opening, or a slow burn to detonation?

Thrillers use two types of openings.

▷ *Explosive* openings deploy a high-impact event. Someone is murdered, or a bank vault is blown open. Extreme jeopardy is apparent from the start, and the reader has an event to pin the bad guys to. The fight is on, and won't let up till the closing lines.

▷ *Slow-burn* openings are used where intrigue must be built as much as adrenalin pumped. It's often used with stories that have complex conspiracies; terrible secrets to be unearthed and fiendish plots to unravel. The opening must build intrigue, if the reader is to take on the complexity of the plot.

So slow-burn openings tend to start small. A scene we can picture easily, something everyday. It may be something as low key as an anomaly. Something that doesn't quite add up, or isn't quite right. In the first of the 'Karla' trilogy, a schoolboy notices that his new teacher has a puzzling secret. The stakes become life and death very quickly, but the crescendo is built towards, deceptively and intriguingly, not laid out in the first scene.

The choice of which kind of opening to use is not determined by genre convention. Action thrillers, for example, can use either an explosive or a slow-burn opening. In the Jack Reacher thriller *Die Trying*, the protagonist sees a woman on crutches struggling with her dry-cleaning on the street. He pauses to help her – then a van pulls up, and she's bundled inside at gunpoint. So is Reacher.

It's a high-impact opening to a relatively straightforward conspiracy – hostage-takers who want a ransom for the woman. Unravelling the conspiracy doesn't form the action of the novel; who the kidnappers are and what they want is revealed early on. This novel is all about action, about trying to escape and prevent a terrorist outrage. A high-impact opening sets up a story full of incendiary action.

But where there's a more complex conspiracy, a different approach may be used to open a thriller. In another Reacher novel, *Worth Dying For*, the bad guys run a backcountry town. They've got every farmer for hundreds of miles over a barrel; they run the only trucking business in this back of beyond. If you want your harvest trucked and sold, you have to use the bad guys.

So everyone for hundreds of miles has to kiss these guys' backsides. If the bad guys choose not to truck your harvest, you're ruined. The trucking family take advantage, in all kinds of humiliating ways. Enter Jack Reacher.

Waiting for the next thumbed ride, he's only got a night to kill in this one-horse town. He checks out the only place open, a bar.

It's a dive. There's one other customer, a sweaty middle-aged guy drinking himself under the table. Reacher decides on a quick fix of coffee. This is not a place to while away the hours. He takes his first sip, then the phone on the wall rings.

It's for the drunk guy. Turns out he's the town doctor, the only medic for some distance. But it's just a local housewife with a nosebleed. The doctor settles back to his whisky, and tells the barkeeper to say he's not there.

Reacher puts down his coffee, picks up the doctor's car keys. *I'll drive you*, he says. The doctor thinks he's kidding. Reacher isn't. When he was a military cop, he got called to married quarters all the time, and women with mysterious nosebleeds. They happen because women who are getting beaten up regularly need a lot of aspirin, which thins the blood, so next time they get hit in the face, the nosebleed doesn't stop. *Let's go*, Reacher tells the doctor.

And it turns out he's right. Though it's a plush house the doctor directs Reacher to, the woman's nose was broken earlier that evening by her husband, not for the first time. Now he's out having a steak with his uncles – these are the trucking guys.

Reacher gets the lowdown on the town very quickly, how these guys can do whatever they want and get away with it. Not tonight, Reacher decides. He goes to the steakhouse, breaks the wife-beater's nose, asks him how he likes it, and then leaves.

Naturally, it transpires that Reacher stays a little longer in this town than he intended. It turns out there's more going on here than the trucking situation – a terrible, repugnant, deeply buried conspiracy. And it's because this conspiracy – like all the worst ones – is so well protected and deeply hidden that this slow-burn opening is deployed.

This opening is not slow, by any means. It's full of twists – the drunk is the doctor, the nosebleed is a near-fatal haemorrhage, the trucking guys have a muscle-bound bodyguard whom Reacher must fight through before he can deck the wife-beater. It's full of tense action and surprises.

But it's a slow-burn opening. Reacher simply does what most guys would like to do in the circumstances. He gives the wife-beater a taste of his own medicine. Tells him he has a message from the National Association of Marriage Counselors, then *wallop*. It's a scene we cheer, even as we snicker at Reacher's sour wit. The scene is not twisting our guts, putting life and death on the line. Reacher doesn't urgently need to kill anyone here, unlike the high-octane opening of *Die Trying*. But that novel has a 'simple' conspiracy at its heart. An extremist right-wing militia, demanding a high-stakes ransom for their hostages. A bloody conspiracy, but a relatively simple one. With a 'complex' conspiracy, a slow-burn start opens up opportunities for the author to attack that complexity.

So it proves in *Worth Dying For*. It turns out that the bad guys are up to much, much worse than their stranglehold on local business. The whole town knows about it, but there's a collective amnesia. It's something that's too terrible to think about, so people don't. And they never, ever talk about it.

So it takes Reacher a little while to find out what happens to children there. In a remote barn, when the trucking guys' Cadillacs are parked outside. They exhausted the local stock of children, so started buying them in. Then along came globalization. Now it's a worldwide conspiracy – 'complex'.

The authorial choice of a slow inexorable burn to detonation in the opening of this novel, rather than an explosive high-stakes first sequence, delivers intrigue as well as thrills. The intrigue, and sense of involvement the action provokes, spur the reader to want to unravel deeply hidden and terrible crimes. Yet this 'slow-burn' opening also delivers a brilliantly action-packed and twist-filled sequence. Slow burn, the maestro novelist demonstrates, should never mean slow moving.

Key idea

Whether to choose a *slow-burn* or a *high-impact* opening depends on the complexity of your central plot. If a deeply buried secret needs to be unearthed, slow burn is the first option. *Get in late*, as the maxim says, but start small – for example, a simple nosebleed is enough to set Reacher on one of his most testing quests.

Push the adrenalin where you can through a *slow-burn* opening, but an author must work primarily on creating intrigue, if a reader is to take on the complexity that's to come. A slow-burn opening will give you opportunities to push intrigue, even if your novel is an all-out action thriller.

A *high-impact* opening works best with a less-complex conspiracy, where there's less to unravel. You'll make up for that reduction in intrigue by pumping the action throughout, so hit the ground running. If the stakes in your thriller are to be life and death from the start, experiment with a high-impact opening as your first option when you begin planning your scenes.

Igniting your action

Whichever kind of opening best fits your story, your trigger incident must do several things to ignite your novel's action, and get it burning to its full calorific potential.

First, it must be something dynamically connected to the plot, not something vague or random. I've read far too many 'tough guy' thrillers that start with a random piece of violence, intended to establish what a fearsome fellow the hero is. These openings read like telling, not showing, and are pornographic in effect – empty action intended to provoke a primarily physiological response. They make the author seem a poor strategist, not a tough guy. Avoid inconsequential demonstrations of violence in your openings.

The opening needs to be meaningful. A guy who wakes up one day, decides to quit his job and travel around Asia, gets a cab to the airport and talks to the driver about living the dream – this is not a meaningful opening. A guy who wakes up one day and decides to travel around Asia, and, in the cab to the airport, talks about living the dream whilst taking a baby picture from his wallet and tearing it to shreds – this is a meaningful opening.

Try it now

It can be revelatory to remove chronology from your planning, and look solely at events and their impact on the story. To check that your opening sequence is firing on full power, write it out in a few brief lines of summary, and bullet-point what happens next, in the order it happens in your current draft. Now flash forward ten years, as if your narrator is looking back on distant events, and try that bullet list again, concentrating on logical escalation. Has the order of ensuing events remained the same, or have opportunities opened to move things around? Has the natural tendency to write chronologically placed unnecessary limitations on your story?

An effective thriller opening must upset the balance of the hero's life. Thrillers don't narrate the inconsequential portions of people's lives, the parts where they're more or less getting by – that's the job of soap opera, or literary fiction. A thriller opening focuses on the moment when life is interrupted, and effort must be expended to restore its balance.

Worth Dying For opens when Reacher decides to teach a wife-beater a lesson he won't forget. *Goldfinger* opens when Bond catches the villain cheating at cards and thwarts him; again, something the villain won't forget. *The Silence of the Lambs* opens when the FBI decides, in desperation, to try an unorthodox approach to catching a serial killer – Agent Starling finds, in Lecter, the last thing she expects, and her routine assignment triggers life-changing events.

The immediate consequence to the trigger scene is that the protagonist forms a desire. Everyone wishes to have control of their lives and destiny, and this fundamental human desire can't help but assert itself when threatened. For example, an office worker is required to review the firm's old accounts. She finds a big hole in the books; it's well hidden, but it's a big hole. Doing nothing is not an option. She must either hide the fact that she's seen it, becoming complicit, or attempt restorative action, risking the enmity of whoever's responsible.

The trigger-incident, then, provokes dilemma for the protagonist. Life was trundling along on its familiar track, then suddenly there's a fork ahead. The protagonist must decide which way to go.

In *Goldfinger*, Bond's dilemma is whether to intervene in a petty card-game scam, or continue sipping his Martini and enjoying the view. He intervenes because the scammer is a wealthy man, one of the 'top' people who has everything he needs to win fairly. This chap could buy strategy lessons from the top-rolling poker players in the world, but instead he chooses to cheat. Bond chooses to teach him the error of his ways.

The guy ripping up the baby photo *en route* to the airport thinks he's made a decision to leave his old life behind. But the photo was in his wallet for a reason. His old life is not the kind that can be left behind. His cab ride dilemma is this: *How do I squash down these feelings about my estranged child, and dial back time to when I was a carefree teenager?* We know that the answers he'll choose – booze on the flight, hookers at his hotel, getting wasted on Thai-stick at a full-moon party – won't keep his deep feelings down for long, and we settle-in for a meaningful story.

The trigger incident's dilemma establishes the opening position on the core value. Bond observes Goldfinger's *unfairness*. The story will move on through *injustice*, and *tyranny* at the end of the line, before *justice* is imposed on the villain. The baby-photo guy is at the end of the line already, right there in the cab – *childishness masquerading as maturity*. He's trying to escape his problems in pleasure-seeking, 'living the dream'. His story will lift him out of the end of the line, progressing him through straightforward *immaturity* and *childishness*, before he sickens of how he's living and strives for *maturity*. The basic design of a thriller should hit all four positions on the core value, but it needn't start with the 'basic' position – it can start at the end of the line, if that's the most fruitful place.

Key idea

The trigger incident *must* do three things. It must upset the balance of the protagonist's life, invoking a desire to restore order. It must create meaningful dilemma for the protagonist – their solution will set the story in motion. And it must establish the opening position on the story's core value. If your opening sequence doesn't check all three boxes, it needs work.

Now it's time to examine the page-by-page substance of a thriller, the conflict. From first skirmish to final showdown, we'll explore how to structure conflict to maximize the potential of any thriller story. First let's take a moment to recap the crucial insights about what a thriller opening needs.

Focus points

Get in late, get out early. Open your scene as late as you possibly can, and close it as soon as possible for maximum effect.

Show, don't tell. Readers aren't interested in a character's resumé, but in story.

If you're using surprise, make it a surprise. An opening scene which features a plane hitting turbulence, or an unattended bag on a crowded train, will end either in foregone conclusion or anticlimax.

Your first sequence must create dilemma for the protagonist. Its events must make them choose between the safety of the known world and a leap into the dark.

Make sure your opening sequence establishes the core value, and its opening position – build a solid foundation for your story.

Conflict: A Close-focus Analysis

In this chapter you will learn:

- ▶ *How a bestselling thriller is put together*
- ▶ *Where the author places clues, twists and climaxes for maximum effect*
- ▶ *How each of these is set up and delivered on the page*
- ▶ *How a three-act structure is used to initiate, escalate and climax the conflict between hero and villain*

Conflict is the fuel of thrillers. From first skirmish to final showdown, conflict generates the action, tension and suspense which keep readers turning pages.

In this book so far we've seen how thriller authors create heroes and villains, and structure their stories, to generate the most robust conflict possible. In this chapter we're going to see how it's all put together in practice.

So we're going to walk through the action of a mega-selling thriller, and locate every tool the author uses to generate and sustain the face-off between hero and villain through the novel. Each twist and reversal, every set-up and pay-off, every climax and big showdown; we'll pin down each dramatic moment to explore how storycraft is used on the page to initiate, complicate, and climax the conflict of a bestselling thriller.

The author is James Patterson; the novel is *Roses Are Red*. I've chosen it for this chapter because it's a standout novel by the biggest-selling thriller writer of our time. Its protagonist Alex Cross was already a huge hit with thriller fans when it was published: a black man from the wrong side of the tracks, Cross is a forensic psychologist turned homicide cop, working Washington DC's toughest backstreets and projects.

He's also a single father, a widower raising a young son and daughter from his first marriage, with a baby son from his second marriage. This wife was kidnapped by a psychopath Cross was hunting; she was raped, made pregnant and made to give birth in captivity. This baby is Cross's second son, Alex Junior, and is still in nappies as *Roses Are Red* opens. Cross is estranged from the boy's deeply traumatized mother; he's giving her the space she needs at this point in her life. The last thing Cross needs is another all-powerful psycho at large.

Enter 'The Mastermind', in the first chapter of *Roses Are Red*.

Opening: reader engagement

The novel gets off to an incendiary start. The very first line is:

> Brianne Parker didn't look like a bank robber or a
> murderer – her pleasantly plump baby face fooled everyone.

It's an opening which hits the ground running. In a supremely economical piece of set-up, it establishes that a bank robbery is about to take place and that there will be fatalities. The *where* and *what* of the story are delivered in its first sentence.

The *who* and *when* of the story are set up in the very first word. 'Brianne' isn't the name of an old woman, or even a middle-aged one; the vogue for Irish names is recent. Brianne Parker, we guess, is almost certainly a young woman – and if she is, then the present-day of the novel is now.

The author has deliberately chosen an Irish name to open an American thriller because readers can date it thus. So by the time they've read one single word of his novel – *Brianne* – Patterson has already got the readers involved, making connections, trying to bridge the gap between *set-up and pay-off* for ourselves.

Patterson delivers the payload in the second clause of the sentence. He confirms Brianne's age: *Her pleasantly plump baby face.* An elderly woman can be baby-faced, but the contrast between age and youth will be jarring, not straightforwardly pleasant. Pleasant baby faces belong to young women. Again, we're invited to make a connection for ourselves, and rewarded by the author for doing so. This particular reward is in the form of the line's final pay-off.

A deadly bank robbery is about to go down. We're right there with the perpetrator. *If you want some action*, Patterson reassures his readers, *you've come to the right place.*

> ## Remember this
> The opening sequences of a thriller must deliver escalating action, and escalating stakes. The reader must be involved in the storytelling from the very first words, and compelled to read on.

The trigger scene

The pace doesn't let up through the breakneck first scenes. Brianne's a professional, but the guy behind the job is called 'The Mastermind'. He's told her exactly what to do, and Brianne pulls a gun on a bank teller – and suddenly this baby-faced girl is talking like an executioner from a gangster movie.

It's a big, shocking *twist*, as Brianne's threats crank the *stakes* from armed robbery to murder.

Which makes this the trigger scene of this novel. It's no run-of-the-mill heist but the debut job of a lethally professional team. We're in no doubt as to whom the villain of this novel will be – guys called The Mastermind tend not to be incidental characters – and watch heart-in-mouth as he pulls his deadly first job. *Intrigue* is created, as well as *suspense*, as we read on heart-in-mouth.

Then comes the first big *plot twist*. The robbery goes to plan. But there are hostages, being held by Brianne's accomplice – the manager's infant son, her husband, and the toddler's nanny. They will be executed immediately if there are any problems. So there aren't. Brianne exits the bank with the loot at ten minutes past eight, as per instructions. The rules have been followed to the letter. The robbery is a total success. But it's not over yet.

The plot twist comes in the last lines of the chapter. Everything's gone well. Brianne told the bank staff she had to walk out of the bank at 8.10, and she did – 8.10 and 52 seconds. Then comes the twist's *set-up*, shocking enough that at first we take it for the *pay-off*: 52 seconds is too late for The Mastermind. He said 8.10 precisely.

But then, even as our shock flares, the *pay-off* to the twist comes. Brianne doesn't call in the fact that she was 52 seconds late. She doesn't need to. Not because The Mastermind or anyone else is observing with a stopwatch. She doesn't call it in because the hostages are already dead.

It's a savage plot twist which slingshots the action forward, igniting *suspense*. If this bank crew are this ruthless, how on earth can they be caught? And – more pressingly – what outrage will they pull off next?

Try it now

The opening of *Roses Are Red* deploys intense, high-octane storytelling. When literary agents and editors use the word *pace* in your dealings with them, this is what they mean. So now is the time to see how your own thriller opening measures up to this breakneck, twist-filled opening.

Can you isolate the first point at which you try to win reader engagement? Perhaps there's an unexpectedly human reaction to the events of your first sequence; or perhaps you've used a striking image in your opening, which takes your reader to the core of the predicament your opening action explores. But if you're struggling to find this point in your first scene – perhaps it doesn't come till the second or third scene – then now is the time to see if you can't nail it on the page even earlier. What are the important details of your opening sequence? Write them out on a blank sheet of paper. Which of these might be worked a little, as Patterson uses his opening character's name and its associations to pack a punch into his very first line? Are there opportunities you're not taking?

Introducing the protagonist

In thrillers where the action opens with the villain, the hero must enter the story as soon after the trigger incident as possible for maximum urgency. The *hero* of this novel, Alex Cross, opens the second scene-sequence. An old buddy, Kyle Craig of the FBI, visits on the night of Alex Cross Junior's first birthday. He's come to ask for help solving the triple homicide and bank robbery. The two old friends stand over the cot of Alex Cross's baby while they talk.

Getting Cross involved in the case is a scene the reader expects, so Patterson *dramatizes* it, by showing us the personal involvement that the hero has in this particular robbery/multiple homicide. Standing over his son's crib, any man would burn in his gut to bring baby killers to justice. The hunt for the murderers is already 'personal', we're shown, cranking-up the **stakes** in the story yet further.

Escalation of jeopardy

Now that the hero's on the trail, the thriller author's job is to crank up the stakes, keep the reader on the edge of their seat, and make the villain look impossible to catch.

Patterson powers through the first act with big, shocking twists to keep the intrigue coming. First, The Mastermind kills Brianne and her partner, immediately, while they're celebrating their first job together. This villain uses a new crew for each heist; we realize at once that this will make him doubly hard to catch.

The second heist delivers the second big twist. Again, a bank manager's family are taken hostage. There are young kids, and the author plays exquisitely on our fears as one of the crew plays a game with the toddlers as he duct-tapes them – 'Duck tape. Quack quack.'

The twist here works on a *reversal of expectation*. Because we've been shown these kids in some detail, we think that the author won't be so cruel as to kill them off. We think the excruciating 'duck tape' game will be as horrifying as this scene gets.

We're wrong. Just as in the first heist, the hostages are meant to die from the start. As we reel in horror from the murder of duct-taped babies, the author moves on to the father of the other baby we've seen in the story, the hero Alex Cross.

Core value: first position

Patterson follows the horrors of the heists with a tender domestic scene between Cross and his grandmother, who looks after his kids, cooks and keeps house. The hero confides that his second marriage is over for good; his ex is too traumatized by her horrific ordeal at the hands of Cross's last nemesis to continue the relationship, or look after their baby son any longer. The subtext of the scene is powerful, and clear. If Cross had chosen a career as a regular psychologist, instead of turning his skills to homicide work, then none of this human tragedy would have happened; he'd still have a marriage, and his baby son would have a mother.

It's a powerful *opening position* on Alex Cross's *arc of change* in the novel. This case will test him to his limits – The Mastermind's methods have confirmed that to us already – but already Cross is assailed by self-doubt. He's not doubting his powers as a cop, but the fitness of his career for a single father and family man.

We're not told this explicitly; again, Patterson invites his readers to fill in the gaps for ourselves, deepening our involvement in the construction of his story. But the conundrum is clear. How can Cross hunt psychopathic criminals, who have no compunction in attacking him any way they can, when he has a young family?

The hero: gaining allies

With the hero on the back foot, aghast at developments in both his professional and personal life, the author brings in allies – an FBI team – to help stop the bloodshed.

The Feds are led by Kyle Craig, the guy who visited the hero on the night of his baby son's birthday, but the narrator focuses on one particular member of the team, Agent Betsy Cavalierre, an attractive woman in her thirties. She's the only female amongst the good guys so far, she's attractive and single and the same age as the hero, she has a distinctive name – the other agents are called Walsh and Doud – and she's the sparkiest of the group. We get the feeling we'll be seeing a lot more of Cavalierre in this story. Crucially, in plot terms, she takes our eye off Cross's old friend Kyle Craig, and becomes the focus of the police-FBI liaison, Cross's partner in the case.

Core value: second position

The hero is strengthened by new allies. Cross is no longer fighting the villain alone. This means one thing in a thriller – things are about to get dramatically worse for the protagonist.

After the long first day of scouring the FBI databases for clues, Cross goes home to give his two oldest kids their weekly boxing lesson. We expect a scene of domestic respite, a lull in the action as Cross connects with his kids and salves the psychic wounds of his day's work, but then out of nowhere comes the *mid-act climax*.

Cross's older kids are a boy, Damon, aged ten or so, and a girl, Jannie, a few years younger. They're shadow boxing together when Damon throws a punch which connects squarely with Jannie's forehead. She crumples to the floor, then begins to spasm. She's having a seizure, a serious neurological event.

The irony is horrible. If we've interpreted the scene as Cross trying to toughen up his kids against what the world might throw at them, then it's backfired terribly. Cross's opening position of self-doubt is thrown directly to the *end-of-the-line position*. He was correct to doubt himself, it seems; now his boxing lessons may have killed his only daughter.

Remember this

Cast your mind back to the first chapter of this book, where we talked about thrillers throwing the hero into the flames, then hosing on kerosene. This is what it looks like in practice. The sequence for Alex Cross here is *flames* (The Mastermind's murderously successful first crime) plus *kerosene* (the relentless escalations in the case) then more *kerosene* (Cross's wife leaving him with their baby son) then yet more *kerosene* (Cross's daughter). The story is burning furiously already, but – as we'll see – the author has plenty more in store.

Paramedics arrive and whisk the little girl away for tests, and immediately she has another seizure. Even worse this time. From a negative opening position, self-doubt, on his *core value* of 'self-belief', Cross's *character arc* reaches its lowest point here – self-blame. First his wife tells him she's abandoning him and their son because of what Cross's job did to her. Now Cross's boxing lessons for his kids have put his little girl in the ICU. How can Cross possibly catch The Mastermind, we wonder, when fate has cut his legs from under him like this?

First act final escalation

Another bank is hit. As he races towards the robbery, Cross learns he's been sidelined. The FBI are now running the case, Craig and Cavalierre in charge. Cross's input is still valued, but he no longer directs what happens next. The *end-of-the-line position* in Cross's *arc* – losing control of his personal life, having to hand over the care of his seriously ill daughter to surgeons – is followed swiftly by losing control in his professional life. The hero's position, at the very bottom of the bell curve, is restated.

Yet even while this is happening, the *resolution* of the novel is being set up. These scenes emphasize repeatedly how long Cross and Craig have worked together, and how close they are. For now, all we're thinking is that it's good that Cross has a friend to lean on in his time of trial. As seasoned thriller fans, we know that authors like Patterson don't introduce anything that isn't essential to the plot. We figure that Craig and Cross will solve the case together, and that their old friendship will help Cross hold it together after whatever's to come with his daughter. So when Cross begins to work with Cavalierre more than Craig, through the next few scenes, we figure we're just being blindsided – that the twist of Craig and Cross winning together is being set up here. A big twist – a huge one – is indeed being set-up here, but it's not what we think.

Key idea

The ending of a thriller, the huge twist that resolves and concludes the action, needs to be set up very early. The entire novel should build relentlessly to the final showdown, from its first scenes – as, we'll see, this fiendishly plotted thriller has. To emphasize the point, the next sequence opens with The Mastermind, searching a database to find the team for his next job. First, the pay-off about the last heist is confirmed – The Mastermind alerted the cops himself, giving his robbers a reason to execute the bank-staff, and strike yet more terror into the hearts of public and police alike.

This bank-heist goes down with yet another **twist**. When Cross and the Feds arrive at the bank manager's house, they find his wife and baby in the basement, duct-taped but alive.

It's a victory, but in terms of the case a backhanded one. The only thing Cross and the Feds knew for sure was that they were dealing with robbery/murders. Now this third robbery has no murders. Time to wipe the ideas board clean again. The only thing they know for sure about The Mastermind now is that he's winning, hands down.

Patterson rewards us for coping with the complexity here by cutting straight to The Mastermind, in real time. He's watching the hostage house as Feds and more Feds arrive. Then Cross comes out of the house. The Mastermind marks Cross down as his enemy, the guy he's personally fighting in his campaign of terror. So at this moment of utter helplessness for Cross – his daughter seriously ill in hospital, his high-pressure case creating screaming headlines while his investigative position gets weaker and weaker – the Villain singles him out and decides it's time to *make it personal*. Once again, *escalation* is relentlessly deployed, cranking yet further both the stakes and the *jeopardy*.

To complete the scene sequence, the author hoses on yet more kerosene. Later, at the hospital, Cross learns that his daughter has a large brain tumour. If they don't operate she'll die, but she may not survive the surgery. The sequence ends with the hero still at the lowest point possible, in both his professional and personal life.

Act one climax: set-up

As the novel moves towards its first showdown, the protagonist is not just 'on the back foot' but struggling to stay off his knees. As a detective, Cross is sidelined and struggling. As a man, his only daughter is on a knife-edge between life and death. It surely can't get any worse.

So it does. Patterson opens the penultimate sequence with yet more terrible news for Cross. The psycho who kidnapped and terrorized his second wife – a man he'd hoped beyond hope was dead – has just struck again. Now this psycho has terrorized his own kids, murdering their mother in front of them. Cross meets his ex, the woman who was abducted by this psycho and made to bear his child, and she ridicules his powerlessness. All Cross is doing in his life, she says, is making personal enemies of psychopaths. Psychos who win, and keep winning. She tells him to stay away from her, and walks out without looking at him.

In the next scene, Cross has to tell his daughter about the tumour. She weeps, and is immediately taken away for yet more tests. Cross has to leave for a briefing of the FBI's special team who will fight The Mastermind. The big news the Feds have is that Brianne may have been raped by her killer, after death.

It's yet another horrible *twist*. When we don't think it can possibly get even worse, it does. Now the good guys are hunting not just a ruthlessly efficient and murderous criminal Mastermind, but a psycho.

Now they know two things for certain. The first is that this guy pulls off the very worst kind of serial robbery/homicides. The second is that for fun he rapes corpses.

Cross's wife's harsh condemnation of his career echoes for us. If The Mastermind is also a psychopath, what hope can there be of stopping him? Any possibility of predicting his actions is negated by his volatile psychology. This wacko could do *anything* next. Yet more awful news for the hero; it seems like it will truly never end.

So in the next scene, the author gives us the first glimmer of hope. He cuts again to The Mastermind, unable to sleep that night. He gets up, then writes a crazy letter to his bank manager about a petty slip-up, threatening the bank and its staff. He signs off by styling himself the champion of the little people.

We breathe a huge sigh of relief. This guy is crazy, for sure, but for the first time in the story it's a weakness. The Mastermind is petty, we see, a fool with a psychotically over-inflated ego. Even when he files his letter away, with all the other crazy letters he's written and not mailed, we still feel sure we've seen the *fatal flaw* in this Villain, the 'Achilles heel'.

Our hopes rise for the hero. Maybe this craziness will give Cross the break he needs. Our psychologist-turned-cop will surely be able to outwit a guy who's mentally ill in pathetic ways, as well as in chilling psychopathy. We read on eagerly, holding our breath for the crucial break in the case.

First act climax

But there's a big river to cross first: Jannie's brain surgery.

The story reaches its *turning point* here. Its genius is that it does it not with the Hollywood suspense and horror which The Mastermind evokes, but with something that happens in the real world all the time. Surgeons remove terrible tumours, and people who were looking death in the face begin a journey back to life again.

So it proves. Jannie's operation is a success. Cross rises from the bottom of his arc. Then, immediately, to make the first-act showdown more of a fair fight, comes the first true *break in the case*.

Cross tracks down a violent bank robber, recently returned to his home turf in DC. Ten minutes later he and Cavalierre have their first solid lead. This guy was interviewed by The Mastermind when he was recruiting for the bank jobs. The interview took place in a hotel room, with the bank robber blinded by spotlights. All he saw of The Mastermind was his silhouette; he had big ears, 'like a car with the doors open'.

It's a striking, original image. It has a touch of jokiness about it, rare in this dark thriller, because we're meant to remember it. It will prove a crucial plot point in the run-up to the showdown.

Key idea

The biggest clue so far in Patterson's novel is delivered with a joke, not with the deadly earnest seriousness we might expect. Big clues in thrillers should never look like big clues.

This break in the case is immediately buried by two emergency situations, both *red herrings*. Cross and Cavalierre find a strong suspect, a redundant bank guard with a grudge, but as they raid his house he commits suicide, surrounded by bankruptcy papers.

Then Cross's second wife calls 911, saying the psycho who kidnapped and terrorized her is in her apartment. But when Cross races there she's alone, with no sign of disturbance – a PTSD flashback maybe?

The question is left hanging, because we're pitched directly into the action of another bank raid, and for a moment it looks like The Mastermind's guys have messed up. But when the cops reach the bank, all that's left are five dead employees.

Act two: escalation and complication

The author marks the opening of the second act with a new level of access to the antagonist, following The Mastermind for two whole chapters.

In the first he's visiting the crew from the last job, holed up in a remote farmhouse. He has murdered them all within a few short lines, but then comes the true horror: The Mastermind strips the female corpse and has sex with it, laughing about how crazy he is. We grit our teeth, remember that this craziness will prove his undoing. We cut away to Cross, as his second wife confirms that she's leaving DC, to try to recover, and that he must raise their son alone.

Then we're back with the villain, putting together a crew for the biggest score yet – the payout on this job will be 30 million dollars.

But there's a big *twist*. This crew aren't so trusting. Two are being interviewed by The Mastermind, but they're wearing wires; two others wait outside, listening in. When The Mastermind leaves, they follow him home. All the way to a psychiatric hospital.

The early placing of this *mid-act climax* comes as a big surprise. It's also a huge *twist*, paying off on the 'fatal flaw' details we've carefully stored away, but putting in question whether this guy can ever be caught. Who'd expect to find a 'Mastermind' in a mental hospital?

The conflict escalates thick and fast now, with the early placement of the mid-act climax clearing the decks for the fight. The *stakes* are given one final escalation, as Cross and Cavalierre are called for a meeting with the Justice department. Big banks are on the warpath – this killer must be caught, now.

Cue the next crime. A tour bus in Washington, full of insurance company employees, is hijacked and disappears. The ransom is 30 million dollars. Any 'mistakes' and hostages will be executed.

The cops throw out a cordon, roadblocks and helicopters, the works, but no dice. The instructions for the ransom come in – 25 million in cash, plus 5 million in uncut diamonds, packed in duffel bags. The Mastermind tells Cross and Cavalierre that they're to deliver the ransom personally, and makes them throw it from a commuter train in a random remote area.

Meanwhile the terrified hostages are still out there somewhere, knowing – like Cross – that The Mastermind kills hostages even when he gets his money. Then a tip-off comes in – the hijacked bus is deep in the woods, near an abandoned farm. Craig, Cross and Cavalierre hasten to the area, find a sentry standing guard. Cross takes him down with a blow to the head, but it seems too easy. *Suspense* is invoked again, as we read on, expecting to see the corpses of the hostages.

But they're inside the farmhouse, unharmed. There's one final *twist* – the sentry isn't a kidnapper, but a local guy who'd been paid a hundred bucks to stand outside the farmhouse for a couple of hours. Another backhanded victory – The Mastermind has gotten away with the loot, yet again.

Second act final escalation

There's a media frenzy around the kidnapping – 30 million is a lot of cash – so for Cross and Cavalierre there's no option but nose-to-the-grindstone police work. They continue to scour databases, and come up with another suspect. A Desert Storm veteran with a very high IQ, implicated in six bank jobs since but never caught. A snitch gives up an address for the guy, deep in the violent east Washington projects. Cross heads up the takedown team – this is home turf.

The suspect is armed and dangerous. Cross faces him down, and wins. But there's another *twist*. This guy has a solid alibi for the first bank job; he was in New York, at a wedding. Dozens of witnesses to prove it. Cross is yet again back at square one.

But the sequence ends with a personal victory. Jannie Cross is well enough to leave hospital. It's a heartwarming scene between Cross and his kids, consolidating the hero's progression through his core values – the time for self-doubt is over. The *personal* journey for Alex Cross is used, once again, to spin the *professional* agony – the contrast between *characterization* and developing *character* yet again put to use by the author in his storytelling. We get the feeling that Cross is ready to win now, and settle in for an explosive act climax.

Try it now

Stakes have been relentlessly raised through the action of this novel so far, but from the start the urgency has been to stop the murder of babies as human collateral in bank heists. The hero's engagement with the quest of the story has been closely tied to his fatherhood of young children from the start also.

Notice how the quest in this novel is tightly tied to the hero's humanity, giving the reader a deep level of engagement with the urgency of the action. Now take two sheets of paper, and on one write a list of potential thriller villain criminals down the page. Concentrate on making each crime affect a different sector of society, and note that sector. Your list might begin like this:

* a corporation whose factories cause birth defects (FAMILIES)
* the 'school-run rapist' who attacks homemakers after they drop their
  kids at school (WOMEN)
* a serial killer who preys on young teens (THE POWERLESS).

Now take your second sheet, and match each crime to a hero positioned
for maximum engagement. The hero hunting the birth-defect corporation,
for example, could be a father himself – perhaps a father bereaved, or
struggling to bring up a special-needs child. Tweak the details on both
sheets of paper, until you find the most powerful manifestation of your
hero or villain. Making the serial-slayer of teenagers concentrate on
gay teenagers, for example, opens up his victim sector to include the
powerless and the marginalized, giving you more options to work with as
you design the hero to defeat the crime.

Second act climax

The Mastermind's crimes have come thick and fast so far. Now
the FBI is in overdrive, with teams searching the far corners
of the databases in shifts, and forensic psychologists busy
sketching The Mastermind's psyche. We remember the 'mental
hospital' revelation, from early in this act, and shiver.

Then comes a big break. A woman claims she met one of the
kidnappers in a bar near the insurance company HQ – a guy
who oozed charm but kept asking questions about the insurance
company. Cross orders a police artist to draw a portrait from
the woman's description. We remember the memorable line
about big ears – 'like a car with the doors open' – a piece of *set-
up* planted long ago in the story, and look forward to seeing the
pay-off this portrait will surely bring.

While it's being drawn, Cavalierre and Cross go for a drink
in her hotel to celebrate. She asks him up to her room, no
strings, but Cross is only a day away from parting company
with his second wife for good. He goes home alone, but this
represents another strength-to-strength resurgence of his
position in the story.

'Self-doubt', the opening position on Cross's *core value*
progression, is revisited, but *charged positively* this time.

Cross's decision – that it's not wise to get physical with another woman yet – is a sensible and manly one, a sign of true character. The hero's resurgent position, we feel, is a solid and strong one.

So the author cuts away to The Mastermind. We're shown him breaking into a young woman's apartment in the middle of the night. He duct-tapes her mouth then cuffs her to the bed. He tells her he's been studying her fertility rhythms and knows she's ovulating. He intends to make her pregnant, and warns her that if she aborts the baby he will find her and torture her, then murder her agonizingly.

It's a grimly surprising *act climax*, contrasting the 'healthy' sexuality of Cross and Cavalierre in the previous scene with twisted sexual psychopathy. The resonance is gut-churning, and our hopes – that the recent upward trajectory for Cross would lead to his first victory – are horribly dashed.

Try it now

The second-act climax is a tough one to write. The first act needs impact and escalation, which the second act must sustain. Then the energies of the novel need to build to the final act's face-offs and showdowns, without getting depleted by the act-two climax or its set-up. This is the tough part – making the second-act climax powerful enough to set the final escalation in stone, without that heft dragging on the pace.

Action thrillers, supernatural thrillers and combat thrillers often solve this problem by using the volatility of their worlds to generate the second-act climax, using something from left field to resonate what's needed. For most other thriller genres, a creative solution is to use a core-value progression to deliver power in the second-act climax – often 'spinning' the value, as with Alex Cross here, by revisiting an earlier core-value position but 'charging' the value differently. Here, Cross's corrosive self-doubt transmutes into the positive realism of a balanced adult, when he takes a raincheck on Cavalierre's offer.

Let's revisit the core-value progression in your thriller for a moment (if you're not currently writing, choose a thriller which kept you on the edge of your seat when you read it).

Take a blank sheet of paper and write out the principal progressions – those big turning points where the core value in the story, or in the protagonist's arc of change, is altered by key dramatic events. Underneath this progression, mark the mid-act and act climaxes of the novel.

Now focus on the second-act climax. Where is this keyed to in the value progression? What's the value being turned?

Now reverse the polarity on that value – if it's a positive value charge make it negative, and vice versa. What would need to happen in the story for that changed polarity to work?

This may be something major, like locating the changed polarity in the protagonist's psyche rather than figuring it in action, or it may be a relatively minor change to the action. Instances of the latter are the ones to think about first, as you consider and reconsider all the options available in your storytelling. A low-key 'trigger' to strong-register change – in the spine of the story, or in the protagonist – can create a powerful second-act climax, sustaining the pace needed to barrel the action forward into the third act.

Final act escalation

The third act is where the author reaps what he's sown in terms of jeopardy and tension, reaching new pitches of horror and suspense as the action powers through to the final showdown.

Alex Cross gets the news about the rape next morning, while the rape victim is in the ER. This rapist referred to himself as The Mastermind, and he was wearing the same mask that the robbers used in the first bank job. This is without a doubt the villain.

Immediately comes another *twist*. The rape victim is murdered when she goes home from the hospital. The Mastermind has fulfilled his threat.

Cross puts in a long day, interviewing hostages from the insurance company. He's beat by the time he gets home. Then the phone rings.

It's Cavalierre, with big news. It's the final *break in the case*, delivered with a huge twist. A 15-year-old girl from Brooklyn has called the tip-off hotline. She can identify the insurance kidnappers – she heard her father and his buddies planning the job, before it went down. Now comes the *twist* – they're cops, New York's finest.

At this crucial moment, *dramatic irony* is again put to work. Cross now thinks that The Mastermind is a cop living with his family. But we know he lives in a mental hospital. We know Cross's search is far from over, but he thinks he's home free.

The evidence certainly suggests it. The detectives the girl has named are from the drugs team, working the worst districts of Brooklyn. They're a tough clique, using their service weapons frequently, lots of disciplinary hearings on their records. Cross interviews the girl.

Her father and his buddies, she says, are bent cops. Her dad has a luxury yacht, takes exotic holidays, dresses like a sharp millionaire. He also drinks and beats up her mom. This girl saw her father stashing sacks of cash in a garden shed the night of the insurance company job.

Her story checks out, and the takedown is a tough, tense sequence. The girl's father makes a run for it, hotly pursued by Cross. It ends in a fistfight – we remember the boxing lessons – they slug it out, but Cross wins. He demands of the bent cop: *are you The Mastermind?*

Final mid-act climax

Back at base, Cross interrogates the head honcho. He's a senior, experienced cop, so he knows he's finished. But he also knows that a plea bargain can get him a country-club prison and a cap of ten years on his sentence. In return he'll give up everything he knows about The Mastermind.

Key idea

The final mid-act climax is a crucially important scene, but pace cannot be sacrificed here. Design this vital sequence for brevity, impact and clarity – detailed explanations of ingenious twists will kill the pace, stalling the motor when it needs to be powering relentlessly forward.

Final escalation to showdown: twists

We think The Mastermind is about to be caught, so the author ratchets up the *stakes* one last time. We follow The Mastermind into another dark bedroom, another early hours break-in. We steel ourselves for another horrible rape.

Twist: the person in the bed is not a woman but a man. *Twist*: it's not any man, but one of the core FBI team – Agent Walsh, Cavalierre's deputy. *Twist*: Walsh is sitting up in bed, with a shotgun trained on The Mastermind.

Game over. The Mastermind admits it. Then *twist*: he draws his own gun, and starts walking toward the bed.

Suicide by cop, we guess? Walsh yells to halt, or he'll fire. The Mastermind smiles, mocks him, keeps walking. Walsh's next warning is ignored too, so he pulls the trigger. Nothing happens. *Twist*: his shotgun is empty.

Twist: The Mastermind knows it, because he emptied it earlier. He tells Walsh that everyone involved in the investigation will die now, starting with him. End of sequence.

Try it now

Note the rapid progression of twists here, the rapid progression of reversals of expectation built from a thriller staple – a murderous night-time visit. Pick five of the most memorable thriller twists you can remember, and write down next to each the thriller staple being worked with. Now take each and look at which variables are being worked with to create the twist – maybe it's a physical thing, like a gun being emptied as above, or perhaps a more subtle way of winning an advantage.

What happens if you change those variables? Can the twist still work in the same way, or does it need extra action to accommodate the difference? As you try this exercise, note how quickly economy turns to all kinds of complication. The key to creating successful twists is to deliver them fast, and as in fast succession as possible. If the twist you've planned in your story creates more 'drag' with its set-up and delivery than it contributes in pace and intrigue, then sometimes simpler twists, which can be deployed in rapid succession as here, may quicken momentum more.

Final set-up twist

Cross arrives at Walsh's house, now a cordoned crime scene. Walsh is in the bathroom, most of his head missing. We realize that something happened between the bedroom and the bathroom. We're correct. The final *twist* to the episode is that there's a suicide note, in Walsh's hand, blaming the pressure of the case. Cavalierre doesn't buy it. Walsh wasn't the suicide type, and the pressure wasn't on him directly.

First thing next morning, they learn that the Justice Department has given the bent cop the deal he wanted, in exchange for information on The Mastermind. Cavalierre and Cross interview the bent cop, flanked by his expensive lawyers.

The cop met The Mastermind three times, he says. Each time he was paid 50 grand for expenses. This impressed him, as did the projected pay-out from the insurance-company kidnapping. 15 million for the bent cops, 15 million for The Mastermind.

The Mastermind's strategy for the kidnap was solid, his information well researched. Most professional of all was the fact that he contacted the bent cops through their bent lawyer. These guys were still in post, still wearing the badge, still unsuspected, but The Mastermind knew all about them. *Twist*: So he must be an insider. Cop or Fed, but one of the two.

But then the final *twist* throws it all open again. Back in act two, at the mid-act climax, these bent cops followed The Mastermind home. We saw this, but Cross didn't. Now the bent cop reveals it to the hero. The Mastermind lives in a mental hospital. Somewhere a cop can't live, by definition.

Story climax

It's match point. Whoever wins this round wins the game.

Cross has finally overcome the novel's first big plot twist – that The Mastermind kills his crews after each job. He has the last crew alive, in custody, and willing to talk. But the two absolute facts they reveal about The Mastermind seem to cancel each other out. They're mutually exclusive. The Mastermind is a serving enforcement officer – must be, to have found the bent cops. But he lives in a mental hospital.

Key idea

The showdown must never be a foregone conclusion. The best thrillers keep its outcome in doubt right up to the final line. This novel shows exactly how it's done, from the very first word to the very last.

Cross has no option but to check the hospital out. Authorities block the police from accessing their vulnerable patients directly, but hand over all the files, staff and patients alike. Cross sets his team to work, cross-checking them all for any possible links to any of the heists. Solid, methodological police work.

Cross and Cavalierre go out to dinner while their teams work the files. It's a flirty scene, building on their last encounter, but it's followed next morning by down-and-dirty realism. Cross and his police partner infiltrate the hospital. Disguised as staff, their plan is to observe the inmates and find The Mastermind. Cross, a trained psychologist, will be dressed as a counsellor, his partner as an orderly. The hospital authorities have agreed to the deal, in the hope this can be dealt with quietly.

We cut away immediately to The Mastermind. He's in his room at the hospital, writing a crazy letter to the landlord of an apartment he's rented. We're reminded of the crazy letter we saw him writing before – this is the guy, we know for sure. Yet still the question hangs: How can this guy be a cop too? He's plainly far too nuts to hold down a demanding job.

The cat-and-mouse begins. Cross begins interacting with patients who fit the only physical description they have – tall, big ears. All are crazy, some are racist too. Cross narrowly defuses violent confrontation.

Then comes another nasty *surprise*. Cavalierre calls on Cross's cellphone. The murdered agent Walsh was one of her key guys – the other is Doud. Now Doud has disappeared. Cross has no option but to continue with the job, the rest of his 'shift' at the hospital.

We cut to The Mastermind, and it's another big *twist*. He's not somewhere killing Doud, he's watching Cross. They're in the same room. He follows Cross along a hospital corridor, and bumps into him on purpose. *Gotcha!* But of course, Cross doesn't know what's just happened. It's *dramatic irony* at its most excruciating.

The action cuts to the end of the day. Cross and Cavalierre are debriefing in her office, over iced tea. They discuss the possibility that the bent cop might be lying about the mental hospital. We know he isn't: *Dramatic irony* again.

The conversation turns personal, as they arrange a date at the weekend. It's another effervescently sexy scene, as Cross reaches the *closing position* on his *character arc*. Personal doubts are banished now; he's ready to get back in the saddle again.

Remember this

A positive position can be achieved on a character arc's core value without that positivity being mirrored in the plot. Cross is still struggling in the case at this point, with a heap of unknowns, one key colleague murdered and another missing, but his character's arc of change reaches positive resolution here – starting with self-doubt, it's ended with self-belief.

The positive position that Cross has reached in his personal arc of change makes us believe that, despite all the odds, the hero will triumph. We *expect* it now – but equally we know that thrillers are all about big *reversals* of expectation, twists. And that Patterson is the twist maestro. We read on, eagerly, the arc's resolution turbo-charging the *suspense* of what's to come.

So the author makes us wait for it, using the only possible delay we'll accept at this point. Cavalierre and Cross go on their date, and spend a pleasant night together. In the morning, Cross has a breakthrough idea. The brutality of the first slayings was overkill that hasn't been repeated. It's the one anomaly in the case, the *crucial clue*. The Mastermind must really hate the first bank for some reason. The two detectives go hit the files.

Sure enough, they find that a former security guard at that bank is currently a patient of the mental hospital. Frederick Szabo.

The hospital has him down as a jobless drifter, but Szabo worked at the first bank in the year before it was hit.

Cross goes back on duty, undercover at the hospital, wearing an ankle holster now. For three days straight, Szabo does nothing out of the ordinary. Cross trains his psychologist's eye nonetheless, and concludes that Szabo is a paranoid psychopath.

He meets Cavalierre. She has the final break in the case, it seems. Szabo was known, when he worked at the bank, for being obsessed with procedure. Everything had to be done his way, exactly to the letter. The other staff mocked him behind his back, and gave him a nickname. *The Mastermind*. Our expectation is led to one final conclusion. This has to be the guy.

The *showdown sequence* begins. Szabo suddenly leaves the hospital. Cross follows him across the city, and into an apartment building. When Szabo leaves, Cross sneaks in and picks the lock of his apartment.

Inside he finds souvenirs of Vietnam, weapons, and crazy letters addressed to all kinds of banks and corporations. Plus blueprints for all the heists so far.

Cross can't believe it. His psychologist's training tells him that no one with Szabo's mental problems could possibly act with The Mastermind's efficiency. We remember that the bent cop insisted The Mastermind must be an enforcement insider, to have known about the bent cops to begin with.

We don't get time to ponder the question. Suddenly there's a huge *surprise* – a tall guy looming behind Cross, with a big knife in his hand. He's wearing the same mask that was used in the 'impregnation' rape, and at the murder of Agent Walsh.

We're in the *showdown* before we know it. The fight is desperate, but it ends with Szabo on the floor, a bullet in his shoulder. Cross pins him down, rips off the mask. *You're The Mastermind*, he gasps, disbelievingly.

Twist: Szabo cusses him out. Calls Cross a fool, tells him he's got the wrong man. And suddenly he sounds completely sane. We believe him. We check how many pages are left – 30 in the hardback, 50+ in the paperback – and realize this story isn't going to end here. The author knows we can 'cheat' like this, and has pre-empted it.

It's a brilliant touch, and our minds race away: Szabo's involved certainly, but suddenly he looks like a patsy. Another of The Mastermind's savagely ironic tricks. We return to the same question we began with – who is the guy behind the crimes, the true Mastermind?

At the same time we realize this, we realize that the 'showdown' we just read was only a taster. The *final showdown* is yet to come, and the *set-up* begins right away.

It's evening by now. Szabo is refusing to do anything but spit at everyone who comes near him. There's no trace of any loot from the crimes at his apartment. Cavalierre and Cross go back to the hospital, search the files for everyone who had contact with Szabo. They identify 19 staff members, six of them therapists. Potential Masterminds. It's late now. They pack up to catch some sleep.

But Alex Cross can't. He calls Cavalierre at her hotel at 2.30 a.m. Szabo has small ears, he tells her. The Mastermind definitely has big ears. We remember that striking image, 'a car with its doors open'. *There are definitely two Masterminds.*

Try it now

In this super-charged thriller, the identity of 'The Mastermind' shifts fiendishly, with successive twists throughout the story complicating and revising the information the reader has almost constantly. This ingenious approach exploits every aspect possible of the basic thriller 'hunt'.

There's a 'hunt' in every thriller, even those which don't feature physical hunts at all. In Donna Tartt's *The Secret History*, the hunt is for which of the group will crack, and expose the buried crime which opens the novel. In William Golding's *Lord Of The Flies*, the hunt is for a way to survive being marooned on a desert island without society's values (those the boys have learned in their short time on earth) causing self-destruction.

Pick out ten thrillers which you've particularly enjoyed, and note the kind of hunt and how it plays out in each plot. You'll see patterns emerge: between types of protagonist and types of 'quarry', between the nature of the hunt and its dramatization. The hunt for a physical quarry (e.g. a fugitive, or a hidden bomb) will use physical action and combat; the hunt for a truth will draw naturally on cerebral jousting and power-play. The exceptions, thrillers which successfully hybridize approaches to the 'hunt', provide valuable insights to a developing novelist working on their own fresh approach. Which of your ten novels uses unexpected routes from hunt to resolution? Read it again, putting yourself in the author's shoes as you identify the choices made to introduce each fiendish development in the unfolding story. Make notes as you go, and keep them for review when you're at the idea-stage of your next thriller.

Denouement and resolution

One of Szabo's therapists has big, floppy ears in his staff photo – his headshot looks just like a car with its doors open. Cavalierre and Cross fly to Florida to catch him at his weekend place, a luxury penthouse on an exclusive island. It's tycoon territory, not the kind of place even a successful therapist could afford. And this guy works in a dingy mental hospital, not in lucrative private practice.

Cross lays it out to this suspect. The therapist was treating Szabo. When Szabo raved to him about a plan to rob a bank, the therapist realized that the plan wasn't so crazy. Szabo had worked at the bank mere months ago, and his plan looked watertight. The therapist decided to manipulate Szabo into taking all the risks, while masterminding a string of incredibly lucrative robberies himself. A true behind-the-crime Mastermind.

Then comes a huge *twist*. The therapist admits it. Agrees that's how it went down. Then suddenly he lunges toward the deck of his fifth-floor penthouse, and dives over the edge.

Twist. A deep swimming pool is below. The therapist surfaces, and begins to swim for the shallows. Cross dives after him.

Twist. The water isn't deep. It's a swimming pool not a diving pool. Cross hits the bottom hard, but then he's out of the water and chasing the fugitive, with the stake-out team flanking him. Soon the therapist is cornered by armed agents.

Twist. The therapist takes a bottle from his pocket, and swallows the contents. Immediately he begins to convulse, then falls to the ground. He speaks five words to Cross before he dies: *You got the wrong man.*

Again. And again we realize that this showdown was not the final showdown. Once again, the author has created a massive reversal of our expectation. The therapist admitted things went like Cross laid out, and we believed him. But we believe his dying words too, because there are still three chapters left.

They're short and to the point. They start by flashing forward three weeks. Cross is suffering burnout from the case. No one can find where the therapist stashed the loot from the last job. It seems The Mastermind is still at large, but Cross has done his best. There are no more leads. Everyone who could've broken the case is dead.

We wonder if the story will end here – with Cross giving up the ghost. But later, at home, his phone rings. It's The Mastermind. Beyond a doubt. He gives information that only The Mastermind can give, then makes a sexual taunt to sign off:

> 'Oh, and have a good time over at Betsy Cavalierre's. *I certainly did.*'

We remember the horrifying rape, the attempt at forced impregnation, in act two. So does Cross. He drives flat-out to Betsy's house. She's in the bedroom, naked, blood everywhere. It's impossible to tell if she was raped before death or after, because her groin has been crudely butchered.

Now comes the very last *twist.* The biggest of the novel; one of the biggest twists in thriller history. The final scene opens. It's just a few short paragraphs long. *The Mastermind is in the apartment with Cross.* Somehow he's standing there, with all the other cops and Feds and forensic technicians. He's brimming over with victory. He's shown them all.

Our minds do somersaults, trying to work out who this can possibly be. As Alex Cross comes out of his lover's bloody bedroom, his old friend Kyle Craig steps forward to console him. He's Cavalierre's boss, as well as a close personal friend. The very last line of the novel is this:

'I'm so sorry about Betsy,' said Kyle Craig, *The Mastermind*. 'I'm so sorry, Alex.'

The *final pay-off* to the story, the unmasking of the true villain, is held back to the very last words of this truly end-of-the-line thriller.

In the next chapter, we'll look in detail at the techniques the author uses in this blockbusting novel, analysing the twists, escalations and face-offs which make for a truly page-turning thriller. First let's recap the key ideas to take forward:

Focus points

Escalation is key to edge-of-seat thrillers. Kerosene is dumped on the flames, then more kerosene, then yet more.

Nothing should be in a thriller that isn't either set-up, kerosene, or pay-off.

Patterns of set-up and pay-off are used throughout a thriller, from a set-up line delivering a pay-off in the next sentence, to a clue in the first act setting up a pay-off in the final showdown.

Big clues and breaks in the case should never be straightforward. They should never come until the story can't progress without them, and should either come with a big twist – the insurance-job perps are police detectives – or come in disguise (one of the biggest clues in this thriller is delivered with a jokey line about big ears).

A high-impact personal journey for the hero, and a high-impact plot, should be designed to turbo-charge each other. In this novel, catastrophes in the personal story (the boxing-lesson, the tumour) resonated the awfulness of Cross's position in the plot. Then the personal story provided much-needed victories (the successful brain surgery) while the villain was still relentlessly all-powerful in the main plot. Throughout a thriller, a personal arc can be used to resonate and escalate the plot.

Conflict – Part Two

In this chapter you will learn:

▶ *The specific dramatic tasks that each act of a thriller must accomplish*

▶ *How what's at stake in a thriller is constantly escalated by the action*

▶ *How plot twists are constructed and delivered on the page*

▶ *About the three levels of conflict, which complicate and resolve thrilling stories*

Act one conflict – choices and tools

OPENING AND TRIGGER SCENE

The first act's conflict is decided by the kind of opening it deploys. As we've seen, the choice of a *slow-burn* or *high-impact* opening depends upon whether the conspiracy of the novel is simple or complex.

Roses Are Red uses a high-impact opening – a murderous heist and hostage situation – because the novel has a 'simple' conspiracy. The villain hires successive crews of robbers; simple enough.

It's the optimal choice for the story which follows. Big twists will be generated later on by complicating the identity of The Mastermind, so the conspiracy needs to be simple for those twists to work to full effect. A complex conspiracy would stop these twists from standing out as powerfully as they need to – so the authorial choices here are a simple conspiracy, and a high-impact opening. The author's plans for the end of the novel decide its beginning.

Remember this

A thriller should *never* be attempted by simply creating an exciting first scene, then 'winging it' from there. This is why most budding authors don't get deals for their books – lack of planning, which translates on the page as poor pace and insufficient intrigue. For a thriller to achieve its dramatic potential, the opening should be intimately related both to the nature of the forces of antagonism – whether the conspiracy is simple or complex – and to the means by which this antagonism will be overcome at the climax. The ending and the 'middle' of the book must be decided upon before the opening is designed.

READER INVOLVEMENT AND THE 'STAKES'

The other big dramatic task of a thriller opening is, of course, to get the reader involved in the story. In the analysis of the opening of *Roses Are Red*, we saw how Patterson uses the very first word of the novel to start the reader making deductions and getting involved with what's on the page. It's notable how Patterson uses extreme *brevity* here – the very first sentence gets the reader working with the text, involved in a compelling plot from the very first lines.

But a simple conspiracy should never mean a simple plot in a thriller, so the *twists* come thick and fast in the opening scenes of *Roses Are Red*. The hostages are threatened with death if they fail to cooperate swiftly; they do, to the letter, but are killed anyway. The *stakes* are pumped up by the robbery, then again by the robbery's aftermath, when the perpetrators are poisoned with pizza. These combine in the plot to make the forces of antagonism seem near-impossibly difficult to defeat, from the opening scenes alone.

INVOLVEMENT OF THE PROTAGONIST

The hero's first appearance in *Roses Are Red* doesn't simply introduce him and get him involved in the plot, but feeds into the raising of the *stakes*. Alex Cross is shown at his baby son's first birthday party, immediately after the murder of a mother and toddler. Cross's complicated relationship with his baby's traumatized mother develops character, showing that the hero is a stand-up guy who tries to do the right thing no matter what – even when it means raising a child, fathered in rape by a psychopath, as his own. His first appearance also shows his investment in what's *at stake* in the novel – a homicide detective can't stand over his son's cradle and hear about the murder of babies, then take a vacation. Again, a single dramatic task of the first act – getting the hero involved in the plot – is used to achieve several things at once.

ANTAGONIST VERSUS PROTAGONIST – PROGRESSIVE ESCALATION

There's typically an alternating pattern in the first act of a thriller, between the villain's actions and those of the hero – some scenes will focus on the former, others on the latter. The hero makes a little progress, the villain makes the job harder.

Key idea

The conventional sequence of events in a thriller's opening sequence – crime followed by investigation of a crime, swiftly followed by escalation of antagonism – has an element of foregone conclusion about it, because we know that the first action the hero takes will not be enough to fix things. This sequence is therefore prime territory for *twists*.

The opening movement of a thriller should show the actions of the antagonist compelling the hero into the story, generating the hero's first counter strike. But we know that this won't solve the case, or there'd be no more novel to read.

So *progressive escalation* comes into play here. Again, it's a difficult-sounding word for something that's familiar to all of us. All it means is this: solving a problem is rarely as easy as you hope it will be, and things rarely go the way you plan. What this means in story terms is that the first action the protagonist takes, to restore the balance of life which has been upset by the triggering action of the novel, is not enough for the job.

CONFLICT – OUTER, INNER AND PERSONAL

Progressive escalation in fiction relies on the *three levels of conflict*. In *Roses Are Red*, the initial conflict is on all three levels:

▶ The *outer conflict* is that there are murderously efficient bank robbers at large.

▶ Alex Cross' *inner conflict* is that he has young kids, and has already seen his family torn apart by a killer he was hunting – how can he risk it happening again?

▶ The *personal conflict* for Cross in this sequence is that Brianne and her partner in the first bank job are his kin. Bringing them down may stir up a hornets' nest of family trouble, not to mention giving rivals or the FBI a reason to sideline him – should a cop who's related to the perpetrators be on the case at all?

In a thriller where the hero doesn't arc, as in the 'modern-day Robin Hood' Jack Reacher stories, there is no inner conflict. Reacher is an action hero, so his adventures push personal conflict – for example, with a Fed in *The Visitor* (USA: *Running Blind*) – alongside the central 'outer conflict' with the villain. In thrillers where the hero does arc, like Alex Cross's adventures or *The Silence of the Lambs*, conflict on all three levels powers the story forward. In either case, differing levels of conflict are exploited to their utmost by thriller authors to create that rich contrast between *characterization* and developing *character*, and to escalate the action of the story, with conflict fought both on the big stage of the story and close at hand.

Roses Are Red has an *arcing protagonist*, so inner conflict is used to establish the opening position on the hero's *arc of change*. As discussed in the last chapter, Cross's opening position is self-doubt; in this story of a mastermind villain pushing cops to the end of the line, the first mid-act climax escalates and redoubles that opening position.

Act one mid-act climax

The nature of this key sequence depends upon the protagonist's opening position. If it's positive, then this big scene will undercut the hero, chopping his legs out from beneath him. If the opening position is negative, then the mid-act climax is used either for a 'false victory', setting the hero up for a big fall; or to pump the stakes yet higher, with another victory for the villain.

In *Roses Are Red* it's the latter, but because Cross is a cop, this escalation has one positive outcome – it brings him *allies*, in the form of Betsy Cavalierre and the rest of the FBI team. This opens up possibilities for the author: Cavalierre will be used both to help progress Cross along his personal *arc of change*, but also to open opportunities for the villain to strike directly and with mortal force at the protagonist, whilst allowing the protagonist to continue in the investigation. In act three, Cavalierre will be horribly raped and murdered, but – unlike an attack on his own person or family – Cross will be able to continue the investigation afterward, with desire for *personal vengeance* redoubling his determination to catch the villain.

The mid-act climax of the first act isn't confined to the villain – it also encompasses Cross's family, with the sudden collapse of his daughter during the boxing-lesson. Cross's worst fear is realized, but not in the way he expected – his inner fear at this point is that this psycho nemesis will threaten his family, just as the last psycho nemesis he was hunting terrorized his wife and made her bear his child.

A big threat to his family comes crashing into the story at this point, but not in the way Cross feared – the danger is not from a psychopath but from rogue cells in his daughter's brain. *Surprise* is used to turn a 'predictable' sequence – another victory for The Mastermind – into one of mortal fear and suspense. It's also a big *twist* on the other development of the sequence for Cross – just when *allies* have arrived to strengthen his position, family crisis overwhelms him.

Hero's position at first act climax

The sequences between the first mid-act climax and the act climax rarely proceed smoothly for the hero in a thriller. If the action is to go to the end of the line, then it's unlikely that the hero will be on a positive roll at this point – unless of course the mid-act climax was a 'false victory', setting up a first act climax of shocking, seemingly irretrievable defeat.

In *Roses Are Red* these sequences are the low-point for Cross. He has to hand over control of his daughter's care to surgeons, while her life hangs in the balance; professionally he's sidelined, with the FBI taking over the investigation. The one crumb of comfort for Cross – that the FBI agent heading the investigation is Kyle Craig, a close personal friend – is, as we've seen, setting up the thriller's final, savage twist.

Act one climax – set-up and pay-off

If the act climax is to be a victory for the hero then it's typically set up by a succession of defeats. If it's to be a victory for the villain, then it's usually set up by an improvement in the hero's position, a feeling that the tide is finally turning, before the act climax savagely re-emphasizes the villain's power.

Roses Are Red uses the latter. Surgeons remove the tumour from Cross's daughter, and the prognosis is good – her life is no longer hanging in the balance. Then comes the first real *break in the case*, a clue to what the villain looks like (his big ears). But the upward tempo is moderated by a reminder of bad times – his ex-wife's insistence that her rapist and kidnapper is terrorizing her again. This element of *personal* jeopardy is setting up the act climax – another robbery, with all the hostages murdered bar one. This survivor is left alive solely to deliver a message aimed *personally* at the hero and his allies. Cross's greatest professional fear – that another psycho will strike at his family – is finally confirmed, capping off an act that's moved relentlessly toward this conclusion.

Act two conflict – choices, tools and pitfalls

PLOT: TURNING-POINTS

In *Roses Are Red* the successful brain surgery marks the beginning of an upward trajectory for the hero. It was set up by the first hint of weakness in The Mastermind – just before the surgery, a cut scene showed us the villain writing crazy letters. We realized that this craziness might be his undoing, and the opening of act two delivers the pay-off.

This is an *escalation* from the 'petty' craziness of crank letters – the villain poisons another bank crew with pizza, but this time we're shown what was off-screen in the first poisoning. The villain rapes the female robber's corpse 'on-camera', and his craziness acquires a new level of meaning. Where the crank letters emphasized a petty aspect to the villain's madness, making us hope that it'll prove a weakness, this time the insane actions arouse quite different emotions – revulsion and fear.

These strong negative emotions provoke the opposite effect to the first confirmation of The Mastermind's madness; now we fear that the villain's psychopathy will make him harder to catch, not easier. Note that this big turnaround in our feelings, this big twist of our guts, is achieved not with new information – we've known since the first robbery that The Mastermind rapes corpses – but with a new way of presenting that information. Where the first time it happened off-screen, this time it's shown in horrible detail, thwarting our positive feelings.

Key idea

Twists are reversals of expectation. The set-up of a twist leads our expectations in one direction; the pay-off sharply reverses it. Twists are often misunderstood as being 'new information in the plot – this twist of Patterson's shows that the *presentation* of information is what's key in a twist, not whether it's 'new'.

ACT TWO COMPLICATION

Having begun on an upward trajectory – from bumping along the bottom late in the first act – act two complicates and escalates matters. Because the conflict must go to the end of the line in a thriller, to absolute extremes of jeopardy and danger, act two's job is to make things much tougher than they already are.

In *The Silence of the Lambs*, the second act shows us exactly how psychopathic the villain is, even while Lecter begins to dismantle Starling's sense of self. In a less blood-and-guts thriller, like Elmore Leonard's *Out Of Sight*, act two shows us a cop and fugitive robber trying to get the one thing they absolutely can't have – each other. Whatever the situation of a thriller, act two complicates it.

Try it now

Pick a thriller from your bookshelves. Scan through the opening sequences to re-acquaint yourself with the action, then see if you can locate the mid-act climax of the first act, and it's act climax. Typically you'll be looking for a tightly narrated important sequence that evokes powerful responses in a reader, followed by a shift in tone and pace. Now see if you can find the act two mid-act and act climaxes, using the same technique. Where are the devilish complications of the plot? Are they clustered primarily in the second act? If not, your chosen thriller is the exception that proves the rule; some thrillers, of course, use the convention to blindside a reader, making their second acts relatively plain sailing – only to bring things crashing down, so that at the start of act three victory for the protagonist looks less likely than ever, creating intrigue and suspense.

In *Roses Are Red*, the second-act complications twist the story, then twist it again and again. The villain pulls 'the big score', the one that most villains would retire on, and though it delivers the big break in the case – a hurt daughter turning in her bent-cop father, someone who's worked closely with The Mastermind and is willing to talk for a plea deal – the information the bent cop gives seems to cancel itself out. We learn that The Mastermind is both a serving enforcement officer *and* a resident of a mental institution.

It's important to reward the reader in act two – there must be the first inklings of a solution to the big mystery – but the action still has to go to the end of the line, so this solution can't conclude the case yet. The *three levels of conflict* are used to push the action to its utmost. In *Tinker Tailor Soldier Spy* we learn that the operative shot in the back before the opening of act one was indeed betrayed, and that there's a double agent at work – the action of this novel's act two sets up a terrible dilemma for Smiley, conflict flaring on all three levels, as he's forced to begin investigating his closest friends and professional colleagues for barely credible betrayals. In Elmore Leonard's *Rum Punch*, compromised smuggler Jackie Brown must find a way to escape both the gun runner who's trying to kill her and the ATF agents who aim to use her to catch him – 'outer' and 'personal' conflict pushing the action towards the supreme effort of will Jackie Brown needs, if she's to escape both with her life and with 'true' justice keeping her sense of self intact.

Act two climax – the slingshot

The second act's final sequence is arguably the most important in a thriller. It's certainly one of the hardest to write – novels are long and arduous tests of writing stamina and, with the crucial events of act three still to realize, the temptation to write this sequence quickly to conserve energy, then maybe come back to it when the draft is completed, can seem strategic.

Remember this

Planning is a novelist's chief ally in the day-by-day grind of getting a draft nailed on paper. Leaving gaps in your planning, and 'trusting to inspiration' as you write a draft, is a primrose path – as is 'skimming' a sequence, to come back to when you've finished. Getting it right first time is the solution to the problem every novelist faces – finding the stamina to complete a draft to its utmost potential – and that depends on solid, meticulous planning.

The act two climax must both reward the reader for having got this far, and compel them to keep turning pages into the movement towards showdown. Therefore it must comprise both *pay-off*, of what's gone before, and *set-up*, to slingshot the action forward into its final reckoning.

In *Roses Are Red*, the second-act climax 'pays off' on the madness of the villain. This particular aspect of the story is used for this key scene because it's been a key factor in the *stakes* so far. First it seemed like a weakness in the villain – the pettiness of the crazy letters we saw The Mastermind writing gave us hope that this might be his *fatal flaw*, the self-important 'hubris' which might prove his undoing. Then it was escalated, in the horrible scene where the villain raped a corpse – this big *twist* turned our perception around, making us fear that a detective's primary tools of logic and reason might prove useless against a nemesis so bizarrely unpredictable in his insanity.

Now it's taken to the end of the line. The villain doesn't rape a corpse, but a young woman alone in her apartment. This rape has an abhorrent 'method' to its madness: The Mastermind intends to impregnate his victim.

It's a shocking departure from the villain's project to date, a mind-bending *escalation* but one with a horrible logic. Having pulled off his big score, and stolen enough money for anyone to live in luxury for the rest of his life, The Mastermind's plans have moved from the professional to the personal. In a horrific inversion of the ideal sequence of events in an ordinary person's life – achieve financial security, then use it to start a family – the villain of this novel makes his fortune with murderous terror, then tries to found a dynasty with the same tactics.

The villain is now in phase two of his two-part plan. That there are two parts to his plan is a huge *surprise*, setting-up the ultimate battles of the final act. Yet again the author challenges us to maintain faith that evil won't win out. We turn pages breathlessly into the final act, hoping against hope that somehow this horror can be ended.

Act three – the end of the line

In *Roses Are Red*, the villain's actions reached the end of the line in the act two climax. Having succeeded in controlling the present, he now intends to control the future.

So only now does the hero receive the crucial *break in the case* – and only because it will slingshot him to the end of the line himself.

When Cross discovers that The Mastermind lives in a mental hospital, his only option is to go undercover, and masquerade as a health worker while he tries to identify his quarry. It's the end of the line for a cop, because here he's without a badge or a gun, voluntarily relinquishing the twin symbols of the authority vested in him by society. He's naked without them, and it's emphasized immediately – the first inmate Cross encounters is a racist, who threatens to get physical with a pool cue.

Twists are critical at the end of the line, to maintain pace. The action can't get any more extreme without tipping over into showdown, so twists are used to keep tensions at a raging boil. *Roses Are Red* uses another *pay-off* for its twists here – back at the end of act one, the villain promised to make it personal. Now he delivers on the threat, murdering one of the key FBI people in his bed, having broken in and emptied the agent's bedside shotgun earlier. This pay-off in turn sets up the horrific action of the story climax. Once again, a set-up planted much earlier in the story is paid off where it's needed, and not a moment before.

Remember this

The action of an entire thriller needs to be planned out before writing begins – if planning is neglected, you may reach your final act and find that you haven't set up enough twists and action to fire the final sequences to their full potential.

The showdown sequence, between Alex Cross and The Mastermind, uses the 'deep set-up' technique to its utmost. From the very first scene, the identity of the villain has been held back. Not even the killers who do his bidding know who he is. Along the way, the only clues we've known for sure have seemed to cancel each other out. The Mastermind is a petty wack-job, a crank letter-writer, but he's also a master strategist. He's a criminal genius, but an insane rapist. He's a serving enforcement officer, but he lives on a ward for the mentally ill.

Now these maddening contradictions are finally resolved, in a triple showdown set up from the very first scene of the thriller. In the final escalation, crashing realization follows crashing realization as the action mounts to the most surprising and gut-churning final scene imaginable. There's a final set-up – Cross defeated, trying to move on – before the final pay-off, the true identity of this villain of villains.

But what makes each astonishing revelation so gripping is that we've been wrestling with this question for hundreds of pages now, from the very first scene. Again, it's clear that the action of act one was designed specifically to ignite the final pyrotechnics of this scorching novel.

As it must be in any thriller. The key to making the conflict fire all the way through is to design it that way. Planning is the most important time that thriller novelists spend.

Now let's analyse the final tool of the thriller author, the ink on the page. From hard-boiled to *noir*, and all-action to literary, we'll examine the stylistic tools and techniques authors use to make their thrillers leap to life, line by line. First, let's recap the key principles of conflict to take forward into your writing.

Focus points

Planning is critical to drafting a thriller. Writing the first scenes, without planning the rest of the novel, misses chances to set up action and twists later.

The three levels of conflict – outer, inner and personal – are used from the opening sequence onward by thriller novelists, to escalate both the action and the stakes.

Mid-act climaxes often bring in big surprises from the *inner* or *personal* conflict. Resolving these conflicts can then put the hero on solid ground to fight the big *outer* conflict with the villain.

Twists are reversals of expectation, composed of set-ups and pay-offs. The set-up of a twist leads a reader's expectation in one direction, before the pay-off powerfully reverses it.

Showdown scenes need big twists and surprises, set up earlier in the story and paying off with resonance – solid planning is key to achieving the pace this creates.

Thriller Style

In this chapter you will learn:

▶ *The key choices to make when deciding whether to use a first-person or third-person narrator*

▶ *Why 'fourth-wall' third-person narration is the principal choice in thriller writing, with original examples to show how and why*

▶ *About thriller genres, like noir and hard-boiled, and how their stylistic approaches enhance the telling of tense and compelling stories*

▶ *How dialogue is used in thrillers to serve the story and contribute to the pace*

The narrator – choices and options

The primary stylistic choice a novelist makes in each project is what kind of narrator to use. Thrillers use 'fourth-wall' storytelling, where the narrator reports actions, thoughts and emotions as if from a grandstand seat. The only limit to a fourth-wall storyteller is the 'person' of the narrator: third person ('the hero fired the gun') or first-person ('I fired the gun').

FIRST-PERSON NARRATORS

In thriller fiction, a first-person narrator is almost always the protagonist. This is because a first-person narrator only reports what he or she witnesses; in thrillers, this must usually be the protagonist in order to witness the principal events of the story. There are two main uses of the first-person narrator in thrillers:

▶ A first-person narrator is typically used to involve us viscerally in the protagonist's predicament. Most Jack Reacher novels are third person, but in a select few (e.g. *Killing Floor*, where his brother is murdered, or *The Enemy*, where his mother dies) Lee Child uses a first-person narrator to make us feel the hero's grief and resolve viscerally. This approach builds strong identification with the hero, and is particularly effective in thrillers with relatively limited worlds.

▶ The first-person narrator can be hybridized to build 'dramatic irony', interjecting an occasional third-person perspective in order to slip the reader information which the 'first person' doesn't know. Thus we can watch the hero forge ahead into danger, unaware of the pitfalls that await. Suspense and intrigue are the principal goals of this technique, when it's used in thrillers; often the third-person information comes in the form of a news report or bulletin, or an email between other characters, dropped 'wholesale' into the text. It's a solution to pace-problems – condensing an expositional sequence down to a few lines of urgent 'bulletin' – which can work well if used sparingly.

Try it now

Pick a thriller you've particularly enjoyed from your bookshelves, and reacquaint yourself with one of its key scene sequences. Make notes on what each dramatic development does to the story, or the key characters' positions in it; then map your notes together like a flowchart.

Now change the narrator. If it's a first-person narrator change it to third, or vice versa. Run through the sequence, taking advantage of your change in narrative perspective – how does the action change? What needs to be done differently to maintain the flow of story to the reader? Note the effects of the change on pace and flow particularly; chances are that they'll be negative. But with a little creative thought you should be able to find opportunities that have been opened up by the change – opportunities to make more of line-by-line chances to bring new perspectives and friction to the action.

The choice of narrator is always a matter of balancing one set of opportunities and limitations against another – as I hope this exercise has shown you, choice of narrator should never be an automatic decision, but one whose pros and cons are carefully weighed by an author seeking to maximize the potential of their material.

THIRD-PERSON NARRATORS

A third-person narrator is an 'all-seeing eye', able to rove at will, without being shackled to the hero's perspective. It can move around between key action in the plot, showing both hero and villain as they act and react to one another.

Its principal use is to channel information to the reader which the hero doesn't or can't know, building intrigue and suspense – the technique of 'dramatic irony'. In *Roses Are Red* alternating between third- and first-person narrators helped the story switch seamlessly between crimes-in-progress and a cop racing to the scene, then maintaining pace with follow-through action, showing the aftermath of crimes amongst the criminals while the cop is still catching up with what's gone down, escalating the stakes and building new heights of suspense.

Patterson's novel also shows how a third-person narrator can be used to look inside the mind of the villain, providing inklings of a 'fatal flaw' to the reader, whilst the hero is still struggling with what seems an unassailable antagonist. *Roses Are Red* uses a first-person narrator for the hero, and a third-person for the villain, giving us access to both principal characters. When thriller authors use a third-person narrator alone, we have less 'direct access' to inner thoughts and feelings – yet a third-person narrator can still tell an emotional story for the hero, using the rule of 'show don't tell', as with Clarice Starling in *The Silence of the Lambs*.

A thriller will stick with a first-person narrator – almost always the protagonist – when the optimal choice for suspense and intrigue in the story is that the reader should never know more than the hero. This approach ties the reader's need-to-know to the hero's, involving them strongly in the story's *quest*. It's a popular choice with budding authors because it cuts down the logistical complexity of the story; in planning terms, it means that the author is following a single 'flowchart' for the events of the story, rather than trying to make two or more sequences of events fire off each other.

Key idea

A first-person narrator can seem a less-daunting choice for first-time authors, but it's important that the simplicity of design it affords is compensated for in the pace and sense of involvement in the story.

Narrative options: a case-study exercise

The pitfall most budding authors' first-person narrators encounter is where first-person 'interiority' is used to give too much direct access to the protagonist's thoughts and feelings – all too easily, this can come across to the reader as 'telling', not showing, and thereby become burdensome. Compare these two passages, for example, which describe the same events in a thriller hero's life but use different narrative perspectives:

▶ First-person narrator

I struggled with the case all weekend, working it through over and over in my mind. It made me feel helpless and weak, and though I tried to busy myself with spade and fork in the back yard, by Sunday night I couldn't stand the feeling of impotence any longer. I went to the store for whisky, poured a big dram and drank it down, then poured another and another and another.

▶ Third-person narrator

She laced on her work-boots first thing Saturday, grabbed a spade and started shifting dirt. It was bright and clear all weekend, the first fine weather for months but she barely noticed, heaving clods and rocks over her shoulder as the green weed-tangled yard turned loamy-brown beneath her boots. By sundown on Sunday she had four veg patches dug to the bedrock and backfilled, but when she opened some whisky for a nightcap she found herself throwing the bottle cap in the trash, and reaching for a half-pint glass.

The first-person narrator tells the reader about feelings; the third-person narrator can more readily show these feelings in action. The first-person narrator conveys frustration with repetition – 'over and over', 'another and another' – whereas the third-person narrator shows us frustration in furious physical action. The first-person narrator leaves the reader with little to do except receive information, whereas the third-person invites the reader to make connections in almost every clause, involving them in the construction of story. The first-person passage is shorter, but the third-person has pace.

Key idea

A third-person narrator is often the best choice for a thriller. 'Show don't tell' is more amenable to a third-person style than the direct access of first-person narration.

The big pitfall with a third-person narrator is to over-use its *omniscience* (the 'all-seeing eye' effect). Don't use your narrator to tell the reader what's going on; your narrator is there to tell story. Neither are they there to slip explanations to the reader, so don't ever start a sentence with 'For' (in the sense of 'because'). If you find yourself using your narrator to tell rather than show, then you are cheating your reader – you promised them a story.

Style and mood

The voice of a thriller is usually very different from that of a 'literary' novel. The latter may open with the protagonist heading out on a spring day, and spend several pages describing the exact quality of the light and scent of the air, and the feelings they evoke in the character, stacking-up *figurative* devices like metaphors and similes with poetic flights of fancy to develop a free-form sense of access to the 'here and now' of the novel.

The literary novelist's aim is to create a kind of poetry of description, setting mood and tone painstakingly. There may be no particular reason for a sunny day in the story other than to establish these, whereas in a thriller such an event would be part of the plot – a calculated set-up, with the optimism of spring about to be crushed by a terrible event.

> Dawn broke clear and sharp, making the rush-hour drivers scrabble for their visors as they merged east toward the city, spritzing grime from their eyeline with wiper wash – the cars rolling down the on-ramp were like a pod of orcas spouting, high plumes of spray scattering sunlight in their wake.

There's the same focus on description, and the same use of specific words and phrases for effect, in this thriller opening as in a literary treatment of a sunny morning. The initial word choices – 'broke clear and sharp' – use *onomatopoeia*, words whose meaning is carried by their sound; there's some *assonant rhyme* ('spritzing grime from their eyeline') to zip the line along with a little rhythm, plus a *simile* ('like a pod of orcas'), even some outright poetic language in the closing clause (notice the hissy *s* sounds combined with punchy *p* sounds here, to echo spritzed water hitting glass). There's no reference to spring or winter, but a reader can guess from what's happening exactly what time of year it is. The passage is textured and literary in tone, yet the focus is not on memories of past springs, or childhood excitement at being able to play outside, or how the first day of spring gives everyone a little lift, but strictly on the here and now – on the hungry hunting-pack closing in on the city.

Remember this

Thriller style is part of what thrillers are – and they're rarely concerned with the beauty of life. Thrillers are the art form of dog-eat-dog economies, just as The Blues was the art form of Jim Crow apartheid. Consequently there's little room for 'celebrational' or lyrical prose in thrillers, but this should never mean flat or featureless writing.

Thrillers work tight patterns of cause and effect, so the passage above is not just description but focused description, showing the effect a sudden spring day has upon winter-worn people at the precise moment they experience it – the sudden scrabble around the dashboard for sunglasses, the realization of how filthy the window glass has gotten when the bright light hits it. It's an opening passage, so it's locating the world of the story in time and space – a city at the end of winter – but also setting the mood and focus of the novel; we can tell from the style and subject of the passage that this won't be a story about 'the beautiful people', nor an exotic treatment of the third-world, but will deal with the concerns of the territory in which thrillers are published and read.

Try it now

Think of something delightful. A random everyday thing that warms your heart. Write it down as a short paragraph, focusing on nailing the essence of the situation.

Now use it for a thriller opening. Tie your chosen event to something terrible that's either about to go down, or is already happening at the edge of the frame.

Compare the two paragraphs. Where are the differences? What tools have you used to create different mood and expectation? Isolate these, give each a meaningful name, then tape them up in your writing-space, under the heading 'Scene setting', for reference when you're writing your draft.

Thriller genres

Thrillers are primarily about storytelling, so clarity and focus in style are key. The words are there to tell the story, not get in the way of it. Different styles have evolved to let thriller authors work creatively within the constraints of the task at hand.

Hard-boiled is a style reserved for the toughest and tautest thrillers. The prose is stripped back to bare essentials with not a single word wasted. Sentences are short and punchy, paragraphs rarely run more than a few lines, and punctuation is kept to an absolute minimum. Lee Child is the contemporary king of hard-boiled, evolving a style of very short sentences, often consisting of a single action each. It *might* run something like this: 'He turned. Saw the window. Looked through it. Then squinted his eyes.' Breaking the action down into each component, one per sentence, puts the reader into the character's shoes and builds a punchy rhythm, where escalations stand out naturally. We know that 'squinted his eyes' is about to reveal something important, and read on keenly.

Literary style is often the choice for historical thrillers, which need to use a lot of period detail to build the world of the story; or business thrillers, which use literary nuance to delineate the complex power-plays and personalities involved; or espionage thrillers, which typically use a lot of atmospheric detail – by their nature, spy stories are international so their authors exploit a style which can make good use of local detail and atmosphere. This is usually put to work creating *mood* – a foggy evening in a lamplit European city will create a certain mood – a foggy evening in Baltimore lit by squad-cars and bodegas will create another. In either case, the mood builds expectation in the reader, whilst the atmospheric description creates a cinematic reading experience.

Noir is for many the artistic height of thriller writing. It was a term first used by French critics, to describe Hollywood movies of the 1940s and early 1950s, the post-Depression years of struggle and conflict, reflected in dark stories of ordinary people going bad: *Double Indemnity*, where an insurance salesman is persuaded to scam his own company by a voracious bottle-blonde widow, or

Gun Crazy, where a cowboy gets mixed up with a carnival sharp-shooter and starts robbing banks. These were stories about the contemporary world – *Double Indemnity* famously had the first scene ever shot in a supermarket, *Gun Crazy* brilliantly kept its camera inside the getaway car, on the street with traffic going past the windows, for the entirety of a bank robbery.

Noir stories focus not on professional tough guys but real people, because they're about a very real phenomenon – the fact that everything desirable, even necessary, in capitalist economies is priced out of the reach of those trying to get a start in life. *Noir* spoke to the frustrations of a generation disillusioned by old-men's wars and economies, and remains very current – life is not, after all, getting any more affordable, or less competitive.

A big feature of *noir* thrillers is a strong female character, the *femme fatale*. She's often the focus of the hero's desire – to live the dream now, before he's too old and exhausted to enjoy it. *Noir* stories are parables of desire from societies where the sweet life is attainable by crime or blind luck principally.

Try it now

What's the expectation generated by a foggy night that's lit with bodega-windows and prowler headlights? What kind of pay-off might follow this set-up? What's the expectation generated by lamplit fog in a cobblestone Geneva backstreet? A lamplit Glasgow backstreet? Sea fog in a New Orleans backstreet? In a New York backstreet? Write out a few ideas, then look at how the same conditions – lamplight and fog – create different expectations as the location shifts. Now change the conditions to bright sunlight; winter, then high summer. How do the moods and expectations change?

Thriller dialogue

Elmore Leonard, the virtuoso master of streetwise thrillers, famously said that if any of his dialogue ever sounds like dialogue, then he rewrites it.

What he meant by this is that the laborious, predictable nature of most fictional dialogue, concerned with 'exposition' and delivering information about the story to the reader – *blah* he interjected, *blah blah blah* she replied – doesn't sound much like real speech.

Leonard's dialogue unfailingly has the zip and snap of contemporary chat, though he almost never uses trendy slang or buzz-words. He creates his effects instead with fidelity to the rhythms and devices of real-world speech, the interruptions and overlappings and circularities and stabs at jokes which characterize most actual human interaction. His characters' utterances often start in mid-sentence, or jump onto what another person's saying, or pick up an idea with an interruption and run with it, only to have another character hijack the idea and turn it around. It's much pacier and more involving than the brittle and mannered 'he asked, she replied' structure of most novels' dialogue-scenes, and I'd thoroughly recommend the Leonard novels *Riding The Rap*, *Rum Punch*, *Out Of Sight* and *Freaky Deaky* for a taster.

Stylistic concerns aside, the main rule with thriller dialogue is keep it short and to the point. The dialogue is there to serve the story, not crowd it off the page. 'Less is more' is the principle to follow here. People in tense situations don't wax lyrical, they say as little as they need to.

And people reading about tense situations want to read at speed, so help them. Put the key information in a spoken sentence at its end, and don't use unnecessary verbs or adverbs with the 'attribution' – just a simple *he said* or *she said* when you need to make it clear who's speaking. Otherwise just close quotes at the end of the utterance and hit return for the next line – maintaining pace, keeping it moving on the page, should be your primary concern.

Try it now

Sketch out a dialogue conflict between one of the following:
* a coach and an athlete
* a boss and a worker
* a professor and a student.

The subject of the conflict isn't important – begin at a point where conflict is already in train. If you're stuck, try reversing the expectations generated by the power relationship: make the coach a two-dimensional winning machine and the athlete the more balanced and mature individual, for example. As you sketch, note how the strongest parts of your dialogue don't need attribution or stage directions to carry them; work at resisting the impulse to add these automatically now, and you'll save your deleting-finger a lot of work later.

Only tie physical actions to the dialogue if the body language is important to the story: 'she said, glancing away', for example, could show that the utterance was a lie or something unexpectedly painful. Don't use fidgeting or 'pregnant pauses' just to break up an overlong dialogue scene. If I had a penny for every time I've read *he paused or there was a pause* in a budding author's dialogue, I'd have a hill big enough for a scenic lookout and a gift-shop. If you need a meaningful pause between utterances, then show don't tell.

Remember this

Dialogue becomes slow to read when the author starts putting stage directions into the text – 'she said amusedly' or 'he said, intrigued'. Show don't tell again – if you want to show that someone's intrigued, put the intrigue in the utterance not in a stage direction. The latter makes a reader have to stop, and re-read the utterance, killing the sense of flow and pace you've worked hard to create.

Now it's time to start bringing it all together. In the next chapter we'll build a thriller from scratch, using everything we've learned about the choices thriller authors make in planning their edge-of-seat stories. First let's check over the key ideas about thriller style.

Focus points

A first-person narrator can seem easier to write – we all know how to say 'I did this' or 'I knew that' – but a third-person narrator may open up more opportunities for an author seeking to show rather than tell.

A first-person narrator is the best choice when dramatic effect can be achieved by the reader never knowing more than the hero.

A third-person narrator can give an author more complexity to work with. Two or more storylines can be run in parallel – e.g. the hero's perspective versus what the villain is actually doing – and techniques like dramatic irony can be deployed.

Genre styles – hard-boiled, literary, noir – can be used to create mood and expectation, or subvert them.

Dialogue is there to serve the story. Keep it punchy, to the point, and above all realistic.

Build Your Own Thriller

In this chapter you will learn:

- ▶ *About the choices a thriller author makes in putting together a story*
- ▶ *How to order these choices, where to begin and how to proceed, to maximize the fertility of the choice-making process*
- ▶ *About each of these choices in depth, and the key questions a thriller author needs to ask of their story material*
- ▶ *How to structure these choices for maximum intrigue, suspense and power*

The core value

Which human value is at the heart of your story? Unfairness? Loyalty or betrayal? Fear? Work out all four positions on this core value, and examine them from all the angles – can the polarity be reversed on any? Is it already reversed in your opening value?

THE ANTAGONIST

What kind of antagonist is needed to explore your core value? What kind of conflict is needed to reach all four positions? If the value is justice, then crimes are involved – so is your antagonist a criminal? Or someone seeking to profit from, or conceal, the crimes of a perpetrator?

It's at this stage that a thriller novelist ensures that the design of the antagonist can fulfil the potential of the story. For example, if your core value is *justice*, then the end of the line will involve reaching a stage of *tyranny*. Can your antagonist exercise tyranny believably? Chillingly? Are they powerful enough, and physically positioned, to be horrifyingly tyrannous and get away with it? If not, now is the time to modify or extend the design of your antagonist, so they will push your story to its utmost potential.

If your story's core value is *loyalty*, what's the loyalty to? What kind of villain can most threaten this? *Self-betrayal* is the end of the line on this value. Is your villain positioned to provoke this? Are they powerful enough in a pecking-order to force self-betrayal? Or can that self-betrayal be figured in surprising and intriguing terms, like Clarice's in *The Silence of the Lambs*?

Whatever your story's core value, now is the time to think about the end of the line. Your antagonist must be powerful enough to take the story all the way.

THE PROTAGONIST

A similar process of examination can be applied to the design of a thriller's hero. Again, a novelist begins with the key value in their story. What kind of person can reach all four positions on the story's core value, and still come out fighting? Will these positions be reached professionally, or in their personal life, or a combination of both? What kind of person has the professional and/or personal life which can accommodate all four positions?

Because the hero is the character who will explore the story's core value most directly, it's time to think about all the ramifications of the core value progressions. For example, a good question to ask of your story is whether any of its four value positions are dependent on a certain time of life – on being young and idealistic, or worldly wise and cynical? Is a male or a female best positioned to explore the core value? A civilian or a 'soldier'?

If you choose the latter, a 'big guy' protagonist, is this a cop or other enforcement agent, or a professional soldier? Do they need to be 'off the leash' to unleash the full power and potential of the action? How can you achieve this off-leash position? Is it something that can happen in the normal course of working life – e.g. between postings – or only by interrupting it? Does this interruption derive from the hero's personal or professional life, or a combination of both? Can it be the result of the villain's actions? Or must your hero be currently 'in the game' – can your protagonist(s) have retired or moved on?

If you choose a 'little guy' protagonist, how can you involve them in the extent of conflict necessary to reach all four positions on the value? Does your hero need allies to survive such conflict? Do these allies come from the same place as the hero, or the same place as the forces of antagonism (e.g. if the villain is a gangster, then the hero's allies could take the form of a rival gangster, or a gangster-turned-informer, or a federal organized-crime agent, or an underling seeking to stage regime change)? Is their quarrel with the villain the same as the hero's, or do they have a separate agenda?

You'll soon find, as you begin putting basic questions to the design of your hero, that the questioning process spirals – soon you may find yourself fleshing out your protagonist in detail. It's a process every novelist needs to undergo in designing their central characters, and one that's especially necessary if your hero was conceived by inspiration – now is the time to make sure that your idea is as strong as you hope it is.

The plot: simple or complex conspiracy?

Beginning to design your plot is where you start putting your answers to the questions above together. Again, it's a process of examining what you have from every angle, using incisive questioning to build the core.

So lay out your responses to the above questions and read them through. Are your forces of antagonism looking like a person acting alone or in partnership, or a boss with hired underlings, or a group of people with different levels of investment and involvement? Is your plot a 'local' conspiracy, confined to a certain geographical area or power-structure? Or is it international, or encompassing multiple levels of society, or multiple power structures? Is your conspiracy 'simple' or complex?

A simple conspiracy permits a high-impact opening which 'hits the ground running'. A complex conspiracy calls for a slow-burn fuse, while you set up the complexity to be uncovered. Which kind of opening does your thriller need? Now is the time to begin sketching out ideas for how an opening scene sequence might run, looking for impact and power – and particularly pace – whether your opening is slow-burn or high-impact.

WHAT IS THE FIRST SKIRMISH?

In the opening sequences of a thriller, the forces of antagonism upset the balance of life for the protagonist. The hero must take action to restore that balance, but the principle of progressive escalation in thrillers suggests that this mustn't be a big, drastic, death-or-glory effort in the opening sequence, or it may be difficult to escalate action and intrigue for three acts thereafter.

As a rule, the first action the hero takes is the maximum they deem necessary to restore the balance of life yet – remember, the hero has at most barely glimpsed the conspiracy at this stage, so they have little inkling of the scale and power of the forces of antagonism. You don't use a sledgehammer to crack a nut, as the expression goes, so this first skirmish will probably not push the hero to the end of the line. They may be in mortal jeopardy from the start, but the first strike-back will not the ultimate action possible. A thriller can't open with the hero fighting through an army of underlings and executing the big boss – unless, of course, this boss will turn out to be an underling himself, of a wider and as yet unimagined conspiracy.

So what kind of action is going to be involved here? Is it something the hero can effect from their current position in life? Or will they have to step out of the course of their life to do this, already? If so, how do they plan to get back? And what can block this, forcing the hero to take stronger and stronger actions to restore the opening balance?

WHERE IS THE FIRST SCENE?

As we saw in the chapter on triggers, the first scene must occur as late as possible in the chain of cause-and-effect which ignites the action. If your opening involves a plane crash, for example, start as late as possible – maybe even *after* the crash – rather than in the cab to the airport.

The location of the first scene also involves its location in the world, which will in turn define the world of your story. What are the values in this world? What do its inhabitants consider to be right and wrong? How do these politics dictate the kind of people who are attracted to this world? What kind of people prosper in this world? What kind fail in it? What does that failure look like? How is power exercised in this world? What are its laws – the real ones – and how they are enforced?

PROGRESSION OF CONFLICT

The first action the hero takes to restore the balance of life may provoke response on all three levels of conflict: *outer* conflict, as the antagonist strikes back at this challenge to authority; *personal* conflict, as the hero finds that stepping out of line creates its own problems; and *inner* conflict, as the hero struggles with the psychological consequences of the course of action chosen. For guidance in structuring these conflicts, developing and escalating them, we can turn to three-act structure and its six sequences of escalations to climax.

Dramatic structure makes the task of sketching a story idea into a fully realized progression a practical job, not a strain on creativity. Sketching out your three-act structure now – then overlaying it with your four-part progression on the core values – will show you where to place the key action, and what it needs to deliver, allowing you to move logically from one high point to the next in your design.

PROGRESSING CONFLICT: THE SLINGSHOT EFFECT

Now that you've sketched your principal conflicts – your mid-act and act climaxes – it's time to think about who wins each. Remember that, if your story is to reach the end of the line convincingly and resonantly, you're going to need a lot of 'kerosene'.

This can be a good stage to start building in twists. If your initial plans seem to leave your hero in too strong a position too early, set your creativity to work – how can you undercut victories, or turn them around entirely?

You may need to add complexity to your forces of antagonism here, to make busting an underling into a dead end or red herring, or provoke an unexpected response from a victory – a cop being ordered to back off after publicly embarrassing superiors. Remember, the only limits are those of your creativity, and as you add texture and nuance to your basic plan, things that seem unlikely can be made to seem the only possible outcome by your line-by-line treatment of the material.

Progression of character

If your hero is an arcing protagonist, it's time to begin sketching the full dramatic potential that this narrative technique can distil in your story.

Turbo-charge your plot by using a character-arc to fuel the conflict of the story.

If not, if you ruled it out as too complicated earlier in your design, reassess your material now – have your story elements come together in a chain of cause-and-effect that might permit an arc for your protagonist? Unless you've expressly decided that your hero will not arc – if you're writing a Jack Reacher kind of serial action thriller, for example – it's well worth examining the potential, at this stage, to build an arc in. The possibilities that a strong arc generates, to fuel the power and momentum of a thriller, are worth considering for your story as you move toward draft stage.

In the next chapters we'll look at what happens when your draft is completed. From first contact with an agent to publication day, we'll cover everything you need to know about becoming a truly professional novelist. First let's recap some key points to remember when building a thriller.

Focus points

Building a thriller is a process of making choices in the order that it's most helpful to make them.

Starting with the heart of your story – its core value – rather than with characters, scenes or situations will help you make optimal choices for your thriller as you develop it.

Begin building your villain before you build your hero. Your villain reacts closely with the core value – your hero reacts, at first, primarily with the villain.

The distance between the first scene and the first skirmish can be most of a thriller or no distance at all. Designing your story's core elements before you start plotting action will help you make the strongest choices.

If your core elements don't gel, and your thriller doesn't start cooking like you hoped it would, sit back from the detail and go back to your core elements, and the choices discussed in this chapter – making time for relaxed creative thinking is the key here.

Getting Your Thriller Published

In this chapter you will learn:

▶ *How to know that you're ready to submit your debut novel to an agent*

▶ *The three big questions which publishers must ask about a new thriller – and how to answer them*

▶ *How to ensure that your thriller shows agents, and publishers and booksellers, what they need to see*

▶ *How to be justifiably confident when it's time to get your thriller a deal*

The market for thrillers

From an author's point of view, publishing thrillers is one of the toughest areas of professional writing to break into.

Firstly, the competition is fierce. The potential financial returns of a thriller are much higher than a book in most other genres because, as we've explored, readers respond particularly strongly to novels with exciting plots and compelling characters. So a thriller stands a good chance of attracting readers in tens of thousands, whereas – for example – a literary fiction novel may only be realistically expected to sell in hundreds.

Consequently there are lots of focused, capable and professional people trying to get their thriller published at any given moment. Compounding this, the opportunities for new thriller authors are relatively few, compared to other fiction markets. Because genres like literary fiction deal in relatively small volumes, there are many literary fiction authors being published at any one time. The publisher's risk is smaller, so they're able to take more gambles.

They're helped in this by the fact that newspaper and magazine book reviews focus on literary fiction. One good review might be enough to make a debut novel's bottom line, but debut thrillers are rarely reviewed in the mainstream press. This means that publishers have to spend much more marketing a thriller than an ordinary novel. This marketing spend is primarily aimed at book wholesalers and retailers, rather than the public, but it represents considerable up-front outlay to a publisher. It's a big investment in an author, so publishers tend to stick with a thriller author for several books, once they've taken them on.

So the thriller job market is tight. There are fewer job vacancies for thriller writers around, at any one time, than there are for novelists working in other genres. Publishers don't add to their thriller lists often, but new opportunities arise all the time; for example, if a new kind of thriller hits the bestseller lists, publishers may suddenly be interested in authors whose work has the same kind of appeal.

Remember this

A clear-eyed analysis of market realities may seem disheartening to a first-time novelist. But the industry would not exist without new authors taking the risk, investing the time, and learning the craft. Novelists may begin at the very bottom of the industry food chain, but success transports an author to very different ground.

The three big questions

Becoming a professional author requires a professional approach to both the craft and the industry. Everyone in publishing who deals with new authors – those agents and editors who are prepared to take a chance on unknowns – has a heavy workload. They may see hundreds of new manuscripts each year, but develop just a few. The focus of your professionalism must be to make sure your novel is amongst these few. So where to begin?

The answer is that you've begun already. By reading this book and giving due thought to the processes you use in creating fiction, you've placed yourself ahead of the curve. You've already eliminated the mass of competition – people who write on instinct, trusting to little more than wishful thinking that their novel will prove structurally cogent and compelling.

Using storycraft and structure to ensure that your novel is a solid piece of work places you, as an author, in a different position. And it's one that matters in the business of publishing. By isolating your thriller's core value, and designing your novel to progress it through all four positions – using a three-act structure to deliver all the compelling face-offs and powerful twists that readers expect from a thriller – you've already answered the first question an agent or editor has to ask about a debut author.

QUESTION ONE

Publishing is both a wholesale and retail business, with many complex levels, but its basic economics are of supply and demand. Readers want satisfying books to read; publishers find writers capable of delivering them. So the first question a publisher must ask of a new novelist is this:

Can this author supply what readers want?

By showing due professionalism – by finding out about storycraft, learning its skills and practising them, then putting them to work in a novel designed to tell a good story well – an author demonstrates, in their debut novel, that they have the potential to win and develop a readership.

QUESTION TWO

The next question a publisher must ask of a first-time novelist's manuscript is the most critical:

> Is this author's ability plain from the first page of their story?

The focus of this question is simple business reality. Publishers know that bookstore managers see thousands of new titles a year, but stock at most a few hundred. Sales teams hoping to persuade booksellers to buy their latest offerings know this statistic too; they represent hundreds of titles each year themselves.

That's a lot of new books. So most booksellers have to make the crucial decision – whether or not to give a novel shelf space – from a glance at its jacket and first page. The opening lines are, after all, the part of the book where the novelist's only concern is to interest a reader in their story, so it's a logical place for a bookseller's eye to fall. The ten or twenty seconds which they spend reading constitutes the most important event in every novelist's career – the moment when, after a long sequence of positive assessments of a novel, a bookseller decides to stock it.

Key idea

Your opening lines are critical in selling your book, every time it's sold – from agent to editor, from editor to sales force, from sales reps to wholesalers, from wholesaler to retailer, and from booksellers to book-buyers. If you count the moment when you, the author, persuade an agent to read your novel, then there are six positive assessments of your novel to be made, by industry professionals, before a reader can buy your book. Every single one of these decisions will depend initially on a glance at the opening lines of your novel.

So now is the time to ensure that your opening is absolutely right. That it absolutely showcases the professionalism you have to offer. Do your first lines grab a reader's attention? Do they prove to them, unequivocally, that reading on will be a good use of their time?

First-time novelists often make mistakes in interpreting these questions. They take them to mean that the opening must plunge the reader into an extreme situation, trusting to extremity – of gore, of 'grittiness' – to grab attention. In the first-time manuscripts that I work on, sometimes this kind of opening uses an action scene; often, it's a sex scene. This kind of approach misconstrues why novelists use high-stakes action, and when. A professional novelist uses this kind of action once they've *involved* the reader, so that the reader feels it viscerally.

They feel the g-force of the car chase, the sour adrenalin of the wrenching discovery, if you get them involved in the story first. But if you start with high-octane action, before the reader's had a chance to become involved, then it's just empty choreography. Bond movies get away with it by using amazing locations and swooping shots from helicopters; novelists only have words on a page, so they must use what they have instead – words on a page, getting things moving with rhythm and zing, setting-up an intriguing situation with pace and economy.

Try it now

Think of someone you've known who has seemed like a 'safe pair of hands'. This could be a teacher, or a work colleague, even a boss; or it may be a sporting coach or friend, or a relative. What was it about them that made them seem so? List five qualities if you can. *Knowledge* might be one. A can-do attitude, and the skills to back it up, might be another.

Now think about your thriller's opening, in terms of the qualities you've listed. Does what's on the page suggest these qualities in you as an author? With no doubt at all? If not, rethink what you're putting on the page here.

QUESTION THREE

Once you've applied this rigorous test to the opening of your thriller, it's time to apply it to every other page. The second stage of publishing a novel – having written a draft – is where the author isolates every sequence, scene, paragraph or line which was the result of difficult compromise, and attempts to find uncompromised alternatives.

For some authors this may involve rewriting a scene or two plus a few individual paragraphs and lines. For others it may involve redrafting much of the novel – but it's worth it, if it replaces something weak in market terms with something that's more likely to repay your investment of time and energy.

It's a tough process, but necessary for all novelists seeking publication. Thriller writers need to be especially rigorous. We've seen how tight the publishing market is. An author shows professionalism by ensuring that their *only* submissions to agents and publishers are solid businesslike propositions first and foremost.

This means going back through all the choices you've made in your thriller, and satisfying yourself that these are the best choices you will ever come up with.

To write a novel, often in direct conflict with other demands on your time and resources, is a huge test of character and mental agility. It's worth giving yourself every chance you can to meet this test, even if it involves rethinking your timescale entirely. It is far, far better to send an agent a flawless draft of your thriller than a patchy one which needs a little encouragement and help.

Because the third big question a publisher must ask of a debut novel is this:

> Can this author repeat the success of this book, and develop as a career novelist?

Publishers don't want one-trick ponies. They want authors who can repay their investment many times over. Novelists who know what readers want to read, and can supply it again and again over the years and even decades to come.

Key idea

What readers enjoy, unsurprisingly, is a good read. When they buy thrillers, they go for page-turning stories with compelling plots and intriguing characters, plus plenty of ingenious twists and thrilling scenes and showdowns, delivered with insight and wit by an author who's a pleasure to spend time with. *Storycraft exercised by a trained practitioner*, in industry terms.

What a publisher wants in a thriller is the good stuff. And they make sure it's there, when they read a debut manuscript, by looking for all the aspects of storycraft that we've explored in this book:

Try it now

Check that your thriller draft has all the components publishers need to see:

* a writing style that is both clear and compelling
* a *trigger* to the story which is credible and engaging
* a rich contrast between surface *characterization* and developing *character* in the principal players
* a *core value* in the story, which the hero and villain are intriguing choices to test and progress
* jeopardy which goes all the way to *the end of the line*, as the core value is progressed through all four possible positions
* a *three-act structure* delivering timely escalations, showdowns, twists and re-escalations
* a satisfying *story climax* which resolves the core value progression, and permits the author to 'get out early', leaving a reader hungry for more of their writing.

When you can finally put a firm check mark next to each of these elements, you've greatly increased your chances for finding publishing success.

But of course luck plays a big role for first-time authors. Every published novelist will freely admit that – whatever the merits of their first book – they felt incredibly lucky to get a deal for it. It isn't modesty, false or otherwise when novelists say this, but the truth. Everyone who gets a deal for their novel is incredibly lucky. The odds, for a new author landing a contract on their first try, are very long indeed. To pull it off is a huge achievement, but also a great stroke of luck.

But as the saying goes, smart people make their luck. Thriller authors do it by choosing the genre which allows novelists to demonstrate, plainly and powerfully, that they have what it takes to win a readership. They put it beyond doubt, in an agent or publisher's mind, that they have the skills, talent and clear business head which a professional novelist needs. People who are serious about their writing career show it with the first draft they submit.

ANSWERING THE THREE BIG QUESTIONS

The key to being the kind of author a publisher needs is to be confident of your material. I've seen many hundreds of unsuccessful submission packages, from my work with first-time authors who can't get agents, and they tend to have several things in common. Chief among them is that they will trigger any publishing professional's well-developed bullshit detector.

Unsuccessful submissions aren't confident in their approach, and overcompensate. They are long, often running to multiple pages; frequently the author includes home-made mock-ups of book-covers. Sometimes even a photographic portrait of the author, eyeing the lens quizzically.

This kind of submission makes big claims for the writing, listing recent bestsellers whose markets the author hopes to piggyback. Whoever's being referenced, even if it shows the finest taste, listing comparisons is a poor strategy in a submission. Publishers want original work, not a novel written by a one-person marketing committee.

Even if they don't go completely over the top, unsuccessful submissions tend to over-define the novel in their covering letters. They don't sound confident; the authors get into twists and turns just trying to say what their work is about. This is bad enough at barbecues, when you ask someone what they do and they spend twenty minutes detailing the intricacies of their role. In a submission letter, the equivalent is a description of the novel's content that takes more than two short paragraphs.

To make a successful submission, you need above all else to be confident in your approach. And true confidence only comes from being sure of your position. From knowing that you're answering each of the three big questions publishers must ask of a debut novel:

▶ Can this author deliver what readers want?

▶ Is this ability plain from every scene of their novel?

▶ Can this author repeat this success, and develop as a career novelist?

When you're positive that your draft is answering these questions firmly in the affirmative, it's time to approach the publishing industry. The professional way to do this is to choose an agent and make a submission to their literary agency. In the next chapter we'll look at how to find good agents; at getting the right fit for the career you want; and how to make your approach, with what to include in your submission and how, if you're to maximize your chances of catching an agent's attention. First let's recap the key things to remember.

! Focus points

Thriller publishing is an extremely competitive industry. To give yourself a chance of breaking into it, you must be absolutely sure that your finished draft is your best work.

Your opening paragraphs must sell your novel all the way through the publishing and retail processes. Now is the time to ensure they're up to the job.

Does your finished draft check every box that this book has covered? Remember that an agent must see overwhelming evidence of hard-working professionalism if they're to see a profitable future for you.

Don't augment submissions to agents with cover designs or photographic portraits. They're not what's being asked for.

Make sure you can answer all the three big questions before putting your work out there.

Finding an Agent

In this chapter you will learn:

- ▶ *How good thrillers can fail to get deals*
- ▶ *Why this stage of an author's journey is one of the most important*
- ▶ *How to put together a professional submission*
- ▶ *Who to send it to, and what to expect*

Getting your thriller read

When you're absolutely convinced that your draft represents the best expression of your skills and talent, it's time to start getting it out there and seeing what other people think.

An obvious way to do this is by showing it to friends and family. Many creative-writing tutors suggest this, but I don't think it's a good idea. Your aim is to enter a professional arena, so seeking advice from people unconnected to that profession – with whom your relationship is primarily personal – is not going to get you the professional opinion you need.

Another option is to join a writers' group, if you haven't already. Some people enjoy the support and companionship these local social groups offer, others find them to be too diverse. Even the liveliest and most supportive groups, however, are unlikely to contain an expert on thrillers who can give you the depth of feedback you need at this stage.

The most helpful way to get a solid professional opinion is to use a literary consultancy. These employ published novelists and professional tutors to analyse the work of aspiring writers and provide helpful feedback. I've worked for one for fifteen years, around publishing my own novels, and have helped many writers from first draft to deal; some of my first-time clients have even won top literary prizes with their debut novels.

Literary consultancies offer in-depth, expert feedback geared towards achieving a deal. A good consultant will provide a detailed editorial report on your draft, highlighting its strengths and weaknesses, and suggesting ideas and techniques that can enhance your work. Consultants work closely with publishing agents, and will recommend you as a new author if you seem to have what it takes.

If hiring a literary consultant is an option for you, shop around. Look for the consultancies which have specific thriller expertise among their staff, and proven track records of taking clients from first draft to publication. Don't be afraid to specify exactly which of their staff you want to work on your novel; once you have their editorial report, don't be afraid to ask for further clarification if you don't understand what's being said.

If your funds won't stretch, then be your own literary consultant. Put your draft in an envelope, seal it, and put it somewhere inaccessible for at least a month. Meanwhile, re-read all the novels that made you want to write thrillers to begin with. Immerse yourself in excellence, re-acquaint yourself with all the things about thrillers that speak to you, then – when you've given yourself enough distance – re-read your draft as if you've never seen it before.

Remember this

It is possible to read your own work objectively, once you've created some distance from it. Concentrate on what the words on the page suggest, nothing more. With practice, you should be able to find you can 'disconnect' your writing-head, and read your draft like someone coming to it for the first time.

Now measure your draft up to the novels you like most. Is your thriller covering the same dramatic bases? Hitting the same targets, as confidently and seamlessly as your top-ten thrillers? Providing the same immersion in a compelling story, with regular escalations and face-offs and big jaw-dropping twists? The effort you've expended already may be wasted if you're not brutally honest with yourself here, so take your time and be thorough.

Taking feedback and 'killing your darlings'

Critiquing your fiction objectively is an essential skill for professional novelists. Once you begin a relationship with a publisher, they will expect you to take editorial feedback and apply it to both works in progress and those yet to be written. This advice may well be contrary to your own ideas about what you want to write, but publishers naturally have their own, professionally informed views about what they want to see on their lists.

Career novelists work in partnership with publishers, and part of that professionalism is to write what their publisher needs. The industry is not looking for geniuses, but capable professionals with the clear-headed commercial sense to do what the market requires.

So it's important to develop this skill early. You can give yourself feedback, as described above, or you can get it from a literary consultancy. The important thing is to give feedback due consideration, and make informed decisions about what your work needs if it's to find success in the market.

This may well involve 'killing your darlings', as the writer's slang puts it. Your 'darlings' are those parts of your work which you love. Every novelist has several in any given work. They'll be scenes, or exchanges, or descriptions, which really speak to you. They may well be the first parts of your novel which pleased you, when you first read them back to yourself. Chances are that now they're holding your novel back.

These chances are high, because 'darlings' are in the text for reasons other than hard intellectual graft. They were generated by pure inspiration, perhaps accompanied by a feeling of expressing your core self, not by nose-to-grindstone brainwork. Having finished your novel, you're now in a position where anything that wasn't the result of tight thinking must be viewed as suspect.

Key idea

Learning to step back from your draft and see it as others see it is one of the hardest skills for a novelist to develop. But as with many of the most daunting things in life, it's a confidence issue – and building confidence in your own abilities (including the ability to adapt and learn) is a core skill for all budding novelists.

So now is the time to turn a flinty eye to these special parts of your work, and decide whether they're serving the project of your novel, or augmenting it. If it's the latter, they need to go, and be replaced by something which directly serves the story. It's the hardest part of any novelist's job, but an essential one. The gallows humour expressed in the slang name for this process underlines its necessity.

Choosing an agent: 'big cheese' or 'hungry mouse'?

When you are absolutely sure that the novel you've written and rewritten is the best product that you can show the industry, it's time to start looking for agents.

This is a process which has been greatly facilitated by the internet. The websites of literary agencies list the clients they represent. Find those with thriller authors on their books – particularly authors whose thrillers you enjoy – and make a list. Cross off those agencies who rarely take on new clients, or whose authors are all stratospherically successful, and look hard at who's left.

Some of these will be relatively established agents, some may be young and building their first list of authors. Some may work at large agencies, whose institutions have the contacts and clout to hook up an author with the people they need to know; others may be at small outfits, whose specialism and focus carries equal advantage.

It's a question of whether to go with the 'big cheese' or the 'hungry mouse', and there are no right or wrong answers. I've worked with both kinds of agents, and had mixed experiences with both. A 'big cheese' may get you great deals, but won't have the time to give focused career guidance and support. You may feel like you don't need your hand held, professionally, but problems arise with publishers all the time – your editor may be headhunted, for example, and not be replaced immediately or adequately, leaving your book with no one to fight for the resources it needs through the publication process.

If this common situation arises, your choice of agent can prove critical. A 'big cheese' will have their own relationship with the publisher to consider, which of course counts for more than their relationship with you; a 'hungry mouse' may be more inclined to hustle, and risk making themselves unpopular on your behalf. This may rescue your book from limbo, and get it promoted to booksellers and the media rather than being left to sink or swim.

However, though a 'hungry mouse' may delight in every word you write, and work hard at promoting you, they may not have the confidence of the people who really matter in the industry. They might be able to get you a deal, even a good one, but not have the weight to follow through and ensure that your book is appropriately promoted and marketed. Remember that, at this stage in their career, a 'hungry mouse' will be trying to capitalize on their relationship with your publisher as much as you are.

Ultimately it's a gamble, and a personal decision. You will choose the agent who seems most likely to help your career. The critical factor is whether they see the potential in your work that you've striven to build in. To find out if they can, it's time to submit your work to the industry.

Submitting your thriller to a literary agency

Once you've decided which agents to send your draft to, check their agency's submission procedure on their website. Most ask for a covering letter, and the first three chapters, usually by email. Never send your whole manuscript to an agent unless they specifically ask for it.

Your covering letter must be professional. It must be brief and to the point. You should introduce yourself, state your relevant experience, and describe your novel.

Relevant experience consists of three things. Firstly, education. If you have a degree in a humanities subject, this is one of the few occasions in life where it may prove useful: Literature, Art, Philosophy or History will place you in the same educational bracket as most publishing personnel. Economics, Political Science, Business and Sociology are good too, showing you're someone with the intellectual capacity to work with complex idea systems. If your degree is relevant to your novel – if you're a mathematician who's written a thriller set in the world of arcane financial instruments, for example, or an archaeologist who's written a historical thriller – then it's well worth mentioning too.

Secondly, relevant work experience is useful for a prospective agent to know about. If you've worked hard in your job and been given responsibility, then you're the kind of person an agent wants to work with. But a covering-letter to a literary agency is not a CV or résumé, so don't detail your employment history and responsibilities like you would for a job-application. One or two lines are sufficient: 'I work in IT support, where I began by manning a help-desk but currently supervise support operations, working with senior managers to ensure seamless service to our clients.' This single sentence tells a story of self-starting capability and professionalism, exactly what an agent needs to hear. If you have no relevant work experience – if you've worked just to pay the rent while you write, and neither sought promotion nor been offered it – then skip this part of the letter. Don't claim a string of part-time jobs at convenience stores as evidence of your dedication to writing, even if it is.

Thirdly, if you have writing experience – if your writing has been published, anywhere – then say so. If you've written for a local newspaper, or contributed articles to a professional journal, or had a short story featured in a literary magazine, or written substantially for your student magazine at uni, now is the time to mention it. It's good relevant experience, to have been given a writing-brief in any sphere of publication, and come up with the goods. But if your published writing is a matter of bombarding your local vicar with poetry until he relents and prints one of your pieces in the parish newsletter, then don't mention it. Remember that this letter to an agent is one of the most important documents you will ever write.

Your letter at this stage should consist of one short paragraph. This should say that you're a first-time author seeking representation for a thriller, and briefly reference those parts of your life to date which show professionalism and ability.

Writing your plot synopsis

Now comes the tricky part – the two short paragraphs of your covering letter which describe your novel.

The synopsis must be powerful and short. A synopsis is not an opportunity to write advertising copy for your book, nor to detail the characters and the twists and turns of the plot, nor to list all the things you think are great about it. What the agent needs to hear at this stage is what kind of novel it is – enough so that they can decide for themselves if they want to read it – nothing more.

Try it now

Pick three thrillers which you know better than any other. Write a two-paragraph synopsis for each, covering all the principal elements of the story, without looking at the 'blurb' on the book cover. You should find this exercise relatively easy. Now write a two-paragraph synopsis for your own thriller. Don't worry if you're tearing your hair out in a very short while. Stepping back far enough from your own work to be professional about it is something which all novelists find hard after finishing a draft. It's an important skill, but one that you'll find comes increasingly naturally as you develop in confidence and ability.

Don't start listing your influences, or say things like 'this will appeal to anyone who enjoys a good read', or 'fans of [insert bestselling novelist here] and [insert another] will buy this book in their millions'. Concentrate on the essence of your story. If a busy agent is going to take the time to read it, the synopsis must be short, and to the point.

▶ Writing your synopsis: a practical exercise

Let's look first at a classic thriller's synopsis, to illustrate. A covering letter selling *The Silence of the Lambs* to an agent might describe it as follows:

> A serial-killer is terrorizing a city's young women, holding victims prisoner for weeks before killing and skinning them. After a politician's daughter disappears a female FBI rookie seeks help from a psychologist turned serial killer, serving life without parole.
>
> He agrees to help, but not in the way the Fed expects. He stealthily but brutally psychoanalyses her, helping her move

on from the trauma of her father's death on police duty. As the hunt for the serial killer intensifies, the rookie learns to make decisions as a clear-thinking adult, and catch her killer. As she closes in to rescue the politician's daughter, the psychologist escapes prison and disappears – but he's helped the rookie mature from black-and-white thinking to an adult understanding of good and evil's co-existence. When he offers her a chance to turn him in, she lets it go.

This is the kind of synopsis which an agent needs to see. Note several things about it. Firstly, it covers everything the agent needs to know in two paragraphs. It does not narrate the plot blow-by-blow, or even mention many key events, character traits or secondary characters. There is nothing in this synopsis about fava beans, or skin-lotion, or moth-pupae, or even cannibalism. As we've explored, this story is about far more than its constituent parts. And it's the story that's being reflected here, not the twists and hooks and dramatic features which the author built into his novel.

The plot summary of a covering letter should reflect nothing more than the journey undertaken by the protagonist, the role of the antagonist in the novel, and how it turns out. The summary above sticks to these three points, adding only the pressure – the politician's daughter – which makes this thriller a race against time. It outlines the protagonist's opening position – a rookie FBI agent – and her closing position at the end of the novel, describing how she moves between the two. It doesn't try to say how wonderful the scenes in the high-security prison are, or how terrifying the showdown in Buffalo Bill's lair – these things are for the agent to discover, as they read.

All the plot summary should do, in a covering letter, is outline the essence of the novel – not how it plays out, and definitely not listing the escalations and reversals and twists you've worked so hard to create. Just the essence. If you're unable to get your covering letter summary down to two short paragraphs, on the above lines, then you're not ready to submit your work. Either your novel is not right yet, or you're still too close to it. Give yourself a few weeks' distance from it, then try to narrate your core-value progression in two short paragraphs – then boil these down, and see if you can't get the entirety of your novel into the space allotted, so that it looks like the example above.

If you still can't do it, don't splurge and submit a three-page synopsis. Even agencies which ask specifically for a synopsis do not want to have to wade through several pages just to get an idea of what kind of book yours is. Two short paragraphs, conveniently supplied in a single-sheet covering letter, is the professional approach.

What next?

Many agencies say that they will respond to submissions within six weeks, but if they don't they won't thank you for contacting them and asking why they haven't fulfilled their stated terms. If they're running a backlog, they're running a backlog. Nothing annoys agents more than writers who can't wait their turn. They expect you to have other fulfilling things in your life to bide your time with, not be someone who's in daily agony about the fate of their brain-child. You may well be in an excruciating state of suspense, unable to sleep or eat, but that's not what an agent needs to hear from you. They want to deal with professional authors, not tortured artists.

Send your submission to the first agent on your list, then wait four months. If you haven't heard anything after that time, send it to the second agent on your list. If the first agent suddenly gets back to you, and wants to see the whole novel, then let them. If the second agent suddenly wants to see the whole novel too, then buy time – claim to be rewriting a short passage of your novel, until you have an answer from the first. Don't tell the second agent that you sent it to someone else first, and that they made you wait six months but you'd still like to give them a chance – it sounds unfocused.

But chances are that you will be waiting to hear from anyone for a while. Publishing is a busy industry. The important thing is to keep working through your list, proceeding to each new agent once your designated waiting period has passed. Don't be disheartened if you don't hear back for a while, but do tweak your covering letter to the next agent if you feel you took a risk with the first one you sent out. If you think of a better two-paragraph synopsis, after hearing nothing from your first submissions, then use it on your next try.

If you run through your list of agents without getting a single positive response, then don't despair. Many of the biggest names in fiction speak of similar experiences early in their career. The important thing is to learn from it. If agents aren't interested in your work, then it needs work. If you can't see why, now may be the time to hire a literary consultant.

More likely, you may get a whiff of interest. One or two agents might be intrigued by your writing and, even though they feel that your current novel isn't something they can market successfully, they'll be happy to read your future submissions.

Many budding authors give up here. They're devastated by rejection, and declare themselves unable to contemplate devising a new novel.

This is foolish in the extreme. Interest from an agent is a big affirmation of your hard work, and you should take it as such. Any agent who expresses interest in your writing is someone who'd be happy to do business with you one day. Your job now is to tailor your writing towards what they've made it their business to sell.

Now is the time to look closely at the other authors this agent handles. Read their debut novels as well as their latest offerings, and look closely at the differences between the two – the distance between them reflects this agent's input. This should give you an idea of the kind of writing that this agent considers saleable – your task now is to make your writing fit this category.

If an agent sees promise in your work and wants you to rewrite it, then the process above may be helpful too. A literary consultant is a very good investment at this stage. Their insights and enthusiasm will give you the momentum you need to go back to your novel and get it right.

The final possible outcome to a submission is success. The agent likes your work and wants to meet. In the next chapter we'll look at what happens next, covering everything a debut author needs to move forward in the publishing process, studying what happens at each stage and how a professional author responds throughout to ensure success. First let's check back over the key things to consider when approaching agents:

! Focus points

Before submitting your thriller to a literary agency, get quality feedback on your novel, and action it. The writers agents most want to work with are the ones who have a strongly saleable manuscript, with all the wrinkles smoothed out, from the start.

When you're ready to submit, put as much careful thought into the short synopsis as it warrants. These brief paragraphs will sell your novel from agent to editor to sales team to bookshop to customer.

If an agent doesn't think your draft is quite there yet, don't push for specifics unless they're offered. Get an expert opinion from a literary consultancy – the investment of a few hundred at this stage is well worth the time and effort you've put in so far.

Be prepared to 'kill your darlings' if that's what an agent needs. If the passages which you feel most showcase your skills are holding up the pace or interrupting the intrigue then they're showboating. Thrillers need compelling, page-turning pace above all.

If an agent wants you to move on, and is interested in reading your next project, then that's a success. Very few novelists get this kind of interest from a literary agent. Now is the time to look closely at your agent's existing client list, and triangulate from their thrillers the way to get signed-up yourself.

Agents and Publishers

In this chapter you will learn:

▶ *How to approach that crucial first meeting with an agent*

▶ *How an agent can help you hone your draft for market*

▶ *What happens when agents send novels to publishers, and about the merits of auctions versus focused submissions*

▶ *What will happen next – deal or no deal – and how to handle it*

Meeting agents

Any novelist invited to meet an agent has drastically shortened the odds stacked against them. An agent will see hundreds of new novels a year, but pass on only a handful to publishers. If an agent thinks your novel has the potential to go to market, and wants to chat, then it's time to pat yourself on the back.

However, a callback from an agent may not mean that publication is the next step for you. An agent's primary job is to sort the wheat from the chaff – to find people who can write. An agent may feel that your writing shows promise, and may want to meet simply to encourage you to keep writing and to stay in contact.

So if you're called to a meeting with an agent, don't assume that your book is about to be sold. But do feel – and act – confident and sure of your abilities.

Key idea

Meeting with an agent is a big affirmation of your talent. But agents meet with budding novelists for many reasons, of which encouragement is one of the most valuable. If an agent wants to meet, but wants you to revisit your work, or take its strongest elements into a new project, then don't be disappointed. It may feel a little like completing a marathon only to find that the finishing-tape has been moved another few miles distant, but the encouragement and advice such a meeting will provide – if you remain positive and enthusiastic – are worth more to you at this stage than a deal.

A MEETING OF MINDS?

Stories abound through publishing history of great partnerships between novelists and editors. There are fewer stories about great partnerships between novelists and agents, but it's these which tend to have the most longevity.

The reason why writer/agent partnerships are less storied than writer/editor partnerships is because the writer/agent deal is not primarily creative in nature. It's important to understand this difference before you go to meet an agent.

Agents combine both literary and business acumen. They have an eye for good writing, and spend a lot of time reading – but their networking and deal-making skills are where they make their money.

An agent will certainly help you prepare your material for publication – or give you pointers as to what needs to be done if your novel's not ready yet – but don't expect your agent to be a combination of mentor, muse and literary chum. They spend much of each day negotiating at a high level, and much as they may enjoy literary chat, their role will be primarily to represent you to their publishing contacts.

Working with your agent: taking 'notes'

Appreciating and respecting the job an agent has to do is the key to a successful partnership between writer and agent. Don't look for an in-depth editorial relationship – agents do not have time for this. If they're willing to give you 'notes' – rewriting suggestions – take them gratefully and without quibble. Don't dicker point-by-point with an agent, but instead look at the big picture of what they're trying to say to you. If they say your protagonist 'comes across as a bit wooden', for example, don't press for chapter and verse.

Instead, thank them for the note, and say you'll take a look at that, then ask them for the next note. Inside you may be swinging between outrage and despair – my protagonist? Wooden?! But these are hurt-pride emotions and will diminish very quickly. Soon you'll be feeling very different, and thinking positively about what the agent actually said.

Agents weigh their words. In the example above, you'll notice that the verb form the agent used was *comes across as*. Not *is*. The agent was not saying the protagonist is a dud, but that the presentation could use some tweaking. It may be that the agent is saying that your protagonist seems to exist in the story only to respond to its events in this draft, rather than that you've created a lifeless character, and that a couple of human touches in early scenes or a brief personal subplot might flesh-out this character sufficiently.

The professional way to respond to a note from an agent, then, is to write it down, think about it, take remedial action in your draft, then write to the agent detailing what you've done. If they think it's sufficient, they'll take another look at the draft and, if they like what they see, send it to editors at this point.

Try it now

When you deal with an agent, you are preparing for the actual, real-world marketplace as it is right now. So go to an online bookstore, find the thriller section, and look at new titles, published in the last few months. Now click on 'forthcoming titles' and work through the list. That's a lot of novels, isn't it? And most will look like contenders in a dauntingly crowded marketplace.

This is your agent's reality. Your reality is the special nature of the project you've worked on for what will seem like forever by now. It's important to enter your agent's reality here, and understand the pressures they face.

So be brave. Repeat this exercise in a large bookstore's thriller section. Pick up every title that's faced-out on the shelves – these are the newest books and bestsellers – and take a long, clear-eyed look at the current competition for shelf-space. Nausea and a crushing sense of nihilism are not uncommon reactions at this point, but better to get these out of the way now before things move up to the highest level.

Submitting your manuscript to publishers

It's rare that agents make 'scattergun' submissions to many publishers at once. Typically they will send a new manuscript only to those editors whom they know are looking for this particular kind of novel at present.

It's also rare, from a writer's point of view, for agents to call auctions for debut books. An auction is where a manuscript is sent to editors with a closing-date, by which time all offers to buy the novel must be received.

What's far more likely to happen with your novel is an open-ended yet focused submission to a few editors. If they want the novel, they'll get back when they're ready to make an offer.

Meeting publishers

It's rare that your agent will ask you to meet with publishers before offers are made. Once offers are in, however, it's part of the deal. Publishers will want to see the cut of your jib for themselves, before cheques are written, so that they can make their own decisions about your likely longevity as a profit-making novelist.

First-time novelists understandably get antsy about meeting publishers for the first time. These meetings are a big deal, when you've been working towards them for years or even decades as your writing develops. But it's important not to build such meetings up into something they're not.

For example, it's natural for developing writers to feel, particularly at first-novel stage, that their authorial self is a distilled version of their best qualities – a persona that they can present to its fullest advantage on the page, but not in a half-hour meeting on a dark Monday morning in January. Consequently they feel nervous that their 'true self' is not going to come across in such a meeting.

It's understandable to feel this way, but authors in this position should remember that publishers have done this kind of meeting hundreds of times. They're not expecting dazzling repartee from such a meeting – all they're looking for at this stage is someone with a realistic view of the world and their own place in it, who is prepared to take the role of a professional novelist seriously.

So be cool. Say less rather than more, and don't be fazed by off-the-wall questions. The first thing an American publisher said at our first meeting was 'So, do you have any famous friends?'

It was a joke, it turned out, because he'd just met with another Brit novelist who'd spent every second shamelessly dropping names. He didn't get a deal, as it turned out; I did, but at the time this publisher's first question had me inwardly facepalming.

So put on a thick skin before you go into the meeting – think of it as getting into character, if you want – and be cool. If you're not sure how to take a question, respond lightly for now, and mull the deep meaning later. If you feel like you're being less than dazzling in what you're saying, then speak less and listen more.

You've got a deal/you haven't got a deal

Most publishers make their minds up about a book after meeting the author. If they don't want to proceed, the author will hear about it fairly quickly. If they do want to buy the book, then several weeks may pass before the publisher makes a formal offer to the agent. Be prepared for a few weeks of silence after such a meeting, because very few novels are pursued with a limitless pot of cash.

Most acquisitions are discussed in depth at editorial meetings before an offer is made. This may take from one week to several, as more and more publishing personnel read the manuscript for themselves. Sometimes even a month or two can elapse during this period, so don't despair if a publisher 'goes quiet' after meeting you.

It is possible for books to fall by the wayside during the acquisition process – publishers' goals and business plans change, as do personnel – and if this happens to your book then it happens. You may or may not get a formal rejection from the publisher, but don't take it personally. Your agent will have an idea of what's really going on, but they may not share this with you. They don't want you disheartened at this stage of your writing life, and may simply encourage you to channel your energies into a new project.

If this is the outcome of your dealings with a publisher, take it positively. Publishers are big risk-takers by nature, and sometimes the vagaries of the market mean they need to trim their sails and think twice about new acquisitions. If your deal withers on the vine as a result, then you'll have better luck next time. You haven't got what you hoped for, certainly, but it's important to remember that – should you find yourself in this position – you are way ahead of the game.

In having got both an agent and a publisher interested in your work, you've won a huge victory against overwhelming odds. Very, very few of the people who've completed a novel have had a publisher read it. Even fewer have been called to a meeting with an interested agent or publisher, and it's a tiny fraction who enter the acquisition process, whether a deal is forthcoming or not. If you've made it this far one time, you will again.

But if luck is on your side, and a publisher makes an offer and follows through, then your work is equally just beginning. In the next chapter we'll study what a publisher actually does, and what they need from an author in order to do it well. First let's recap the key points about an author's role in the acquisition process:

Focus points

Your agent is your business partner, not your editor. An agent may give you advice on rewriting for market, if they're interested in developing you as a novelist, but it's important to remain self-starting in this relationship, and read the big picture from an agent's well-chosen words.

Novelists dream of big-money auctions, but open-ended submissions to publishers have the benefit of allowing relationships to develop with the project.

Publishers' editorial meetings are where potential acquisitions get the green light or otherwise. They're complex meetings with all key personnel present, from sales to finance, and if your novel doesn't make it through the process first time it's important to remember that extremely few do.

If a publisher's ultimate decision is negative, the important thing is to learn from the experience. If your agent won't be specific as to why you weren't lucky this time, take it as just that – the luck of the draw. All novelists regard their first deal as the fruit of hard work combined with a great stroke of luck.

If your novel didn't make it all the way through the acquisition process, you have plenty of reason to stay positive as you begin to scout ideas for your next project. Very few novelists attract the interest of an agent; even fewer get discussed by publishers. You've worked your way into the upper percentile already.

Publishers and Other Publishing Options

In this chapter you will learn:

▶ *What happens in-house when publishers buy books*

▶ *Which publishing staff make decisions in the acquisition process, and why*

▶ *About what happens to a book, and its author, once a book is bought, and how to make the pre-publication minefield work for you*

▶ *About other proven publishing options for new authors*

Inside a publishing house

If an editor reads your thriller and is interested, they will discuss it with colleagues at the next in-house editorial meeting.

Publishers hold these meetings weekly. They're a forum for editors to pitch new acquisitions and commissions to their colleagues, and invite their expert feedback.

These meetings are where it all happens. Present are the Publisher, the Sales Director, the Finance Director, plus senior staff from publicity and marketing. Between them, these people decide if a new project has the potential to be profitable – and, in the case of a debut author, if this novelist is worth investing in.

At these key meetings, the editor presents the book. They'll talk about what interested them in the project, its primary features, and give their assessment of the author's abilities and potential to develop as a writer.

Their colleagues take copies of the manuscript away and read them. At the next meeting, they'll give their own assessment of the novel's chances based on their particular expertise.

Often the verdict will be negative. The Sales Director may be hearing from her reps that this kind of novel is not getting shelf space from booksellers right now. The Publicity Director may feel that this kind of novel needs a promotable author behind it, and that the author in this case may not have what it takes. The Finance Director will consider everyone's input and decide whether the price the agent is asking for the manuscript represents an acceptable risk of the firm's money.

There are a lot of hoops to jump through. And if your novel doesn't make it all the way, then maybe the next one will. The important thing is to decide for yourself why it didn't happen this time, based on what you hear, and plan your next project to cover those bases. Some things can only be learned from experience, and a publisher's precise requirements is one of them. But to have come this far with your novel is an amazing achievement in itself. Extremely few debut authors make it to this stage.

Contracts and negotiation

The enthusiasm for a new project within a publisher is infectious, but don't let it distract you from negotiations in this critical period before contracts are signed. This is the last time you will have any traction in your deal, so it's important to pin down exactly what you want.

For example, I usually ask for a bump in my percentage once I sell a certain amount of copies – publishers are only too happy to respond to such confidence, in my experience, and it means exponentially more cash if your book performs as well as you've designed it to. Another good thing to consider is exactly when rights will revert to you. If a few years down the line this publisher has changed strategy in your particular market, and isn't making much effort to sell your book any more, you may well want to sell the rights to a publisher who'll work a little harder.

So now is the time to ask. Your agent is a contracts expert by definition, so if there's anything you need clarified then you have the horse's mouth at hand.

But it's also time to consider your place in the overall picture. Remember that schoolroom poster of the ocean food chain, with whales at the top and krill at the bottom? Publishers are the whales in this pecking-order, and writers are the krill's breakfast. Be realistic in your negotiations, and don't haggle. Ask, by all means, but listen to the answer your agent or publisher gives you, and edit your ask-list accordingly.

Editing and marketing

The next stage for a new author is to edit the novel.

Your editor will discuss with you which elements of your current draft work best, and which may need tweaking to find its full potential. They may ask you to make changes, sometimes big ones. They may refer you to a freelance copy-editor or editorial consultant, and ask you to work closely with them to produce a 'clean' draft for publication. Or they may simply give you a marked-up copy of the manuscript with their thoughts and suggestions pencilled in, and ask you to work through it.

In all cases, consider what's being asked before you respond to each point that's made to you. On big plot points – cutting a character or reworking a sequence, for example – it's wise to listen to the opinion you're given very carefully. It will be informed by the views of many other publishing professionals, and is extremely valuable.

On smaller, line-by-line points, I only argue if the proposed change disrupts the pace, flow or rhythm, and only then if I can't find a compromise. The important thing is to take time to try to find the compromise first. Give yourself a good few weeks to work through suggestions for editorial revision before responding with your considered thoughts.

It's at this stage that the marketing machine will swing into action too. A publication date will be set, and an Advance Information document (known as an AI) is prepared for sales personnel and booksellers.

The AI typically contains the 'blurb' which will eventually appear on the back-cover or inside flap of the finished book. You may well be asked to write a first draft of the blurb, and it's important to get it right.

I'd recommend reading a copywriting textbook or two at this point, if you haven't already. It's also wise to spend some time browsing in bookstores, looking at how the blurb is used to hook attention and hold it in your market. Give yourself a week or two to condense your first effort down into the hard-hitting few lines of text that's needed before submitting your effort. Expect it to change, possibly radically. Your publisher knows better than you what the blurb of a book needs to do, so be as accommodating as you can.

Design and publicity

The jacket design is similarly an area where you must defer to your publisher's opinion. They may invite your ideas, but the look and feel of the finished book will be the result of their expertise and creativity. Knowing what can attract a browser's attention across a crowded bookstore is a retail science, and publishers' design departments work at its leading edge.

As publication approaches, the publicity department will be in touch, usually with a questionnaire. If you have an idea for an article which you could realistically place with a magazine or newspaper – even if it's a local one – to tie in with publication, now is the time to get to work. Research the kind of slots that are available to first-time novelists in print media – articles for the family or travel sections of weekend newspapers for example – and write your article to fit the brief. Only then try it on your publicist – if they think it's got a chance of publication, they'll usually let you try to place the article yourself.

If you have any experience of public speaking or giving presentations professionally, your publicist's confidence in booking you for festivals and bookstore events may be bolstered. But don't worry if a glittering schedule of interviews and festival appearances isn't lined up for you. Your publicity department can promote books in all kinds of ways, and can help you with realistic options for your work – such as placing an article about researching the world of your novel on a thriller blog, for example. Now is the time to think creatively about what could generate an entertaining article.

Publication – reviews, interviews and public events

As publication day approaches, your publicist will be swapping emails with you, if you've built a good relationship, to let you know who'll be reviewing your work and where. You may also get booked for some local or national radio, or to be interviewed by journalists or bloggers. Butterflies at the prospect are quite natural, but look at how writers you admire handle their interviews, do your research, and you'll be in a more confident position.

Reviews may appear before official publication, or several months after it. Good reviews can feel intensely validating, sour reviews can sting. Wise novelists grow a thick skin to both fairly quickly. If another novelist reviews your book, positively or otherwise, it's courteous to send a brief personal note.

You may have some bookstore readings to do at this point too. These are typically in the evening, and usually involve a few authors, often with little in common except recent publication dates. For this reason, you need to work all the harder to make your own contribution a success.

Choose an excerpt from your book which you can deliver entertainingly and without too much preamble. There's nothing worse at a bookstore event than an author who spends half their ten-minute slot explaining a complicated set-up. If you need to tweak your chosen scene a little to cut down on the preamble, go right ahead.

Start your reading with a joke about the subject or world of the scene in question, then segue into a very brief set-up, telling the audience only what they need to know in order to follow the scene as you read it aloud. Get into your chosen scene late, and get out early.

As the date looms, run through your piece aloud several times to ensure you won't run over time. Remember that sales reps are some of the most important people in your career. Even if they're not present at the bookstore event, they'll have set it up – and the bookseller will be trusting to the rep's judgement, that you're someone who can entertain an audience and carry off a bookstore event. Follow the advice above and you'll do fine.

What next?

By now you should have forged good relationships with your editor and their team, and ideally some of the sales reps too. You will have used your contact time with your publisher to gain a thorough impression of their publishing strategies and methods, and be tailoring your next novel accordingly. It's all too easy to bury yourself in the writing and let relationships sit on the back burner, but stay in touch with reps if you can, and make yourself available for more bookstore readings if they ask. You're no longer an outsider trying to break in, you're part of a professional team now. Take your role in it seriously and you can't go far wrong.

Other publishing alternatives

Self-publishing is a viable option for some authors, but newcomers to this area should beware of 'vanity publishers'. These are companies who will praise your work to the skies, then ask an outrageous sum to print up copies of your novel. They may make extravagant claims about marketing your work, but the likelihood is that your book will languish in a warehouse until the vanity-publisher offers to sell unsold copies back to you at an inflated price, thereby gouging you twice for their services. The key to spotting a 'vanity publisher' is in the amount of flattery they lavish upon your work, and the fine print of their contracts – typically in these contracts, rights belong to the vanity publisher, not the author.

There are genuine 'partnership publishing' houses out there, and with the right novel they can do a great job for an author, marketing and publicizing the book as effectively as any small publisher can. Outfits like the UK's Antony Rowe meet the author halfway – they print the book (or set-up print-on-demand), market it to the trade via a leading wholesaler, and help the author find designers and typesetters. But paper and printing remain costly, and print-on-demand even more so. Authors going down this route will find they have a lot of phone-work and admin to do for a small return on each book sold.

Another option is to *do it yourself* entirely – printing, marketing, publicizing. Before setting off down this route, consider whom you're going to sell copies of your book to. You're not going to be able to place many with bookshops, even if you spend weeks cold-calling – and if you do, most booksellers will insist on sale-or-return, so each copy you place with a bookstore may spend a few weeks on their shelves and a few months in their stockroom before being returned to you. This makes both inventory and invoicing a nightmare, particularly for authors who would rather be writing than chasing endless dead invoices.

But in my experience self-publishing is best-suited to non-fiction and novelty works whose title sells the book – for example, Stephen Clarke's bestselling *A Life in the Merde* began as a self-published book sold directly by the author to bookshops over the telephone. It can work for fiction – if you've written a thriller set in a niche world, and you can reach that niche directly, then you might sell some copies – for example, if your story is set in the world of cult-TV conventions, and you can attend these and either sell books directly or distribute flyers, then this may be a worthwhile option.

However, for most thriller writers the publishing industry is the best way to go. If you don't find success on your first try, learning from the experience and tailoring your next project accordingly is the tried-and-tested route to making a living from writing fiction.

In the final chapter we'll focus on troubleshooting problems which thriller writers encounter in the process of bringing a project to fruition. First let's recap the key points to remember about dealing with publishers and self-publishers:

! Focus points

If your novel makes it to an editorial meeting, then it will get the expert attention of many seasoned publishing professionals. It's a huge achievement for someone to make it from enthusiastic reader to budding writer to novelist whose work is discussed in thoughtful detail. If the outcome isn't a deal this time, you have still climbed an awesome mountain to reach where you are now.

If you do get a deal, now is the time to draw on your agent's experience in discussing what's possible in your contract. There may be wiggle-room in some areas, particularly with multi-territory deals, but if there isn't don't feel short-changed. The standard industry contract (with a royalty around 7.5 per cent of publisher's net receipts on the first ten thousand) is a good deal in a tough industry.

As you move into the editorial and early marketing stages of the publication process, it's important to gear up. Read a copywriting textbook before attempting the blurb, learn about the bookselling retail sector, and spend time in bookshops studying current trends in jacket design and overall presentation in your chosen market. You'll need to make informed contributions to the creative process of publication, so give yourself a basic grounding in design, copywriting and marketing.

Be prepared to do bookstore events and readings at short notice, as publication approaches. Have a five-minute and a ten-minute passage from your novel chosen and rehearsed, and start thinking about a joke for your introductory patter well in advance. Remind your sales reps, at least three months before publication, that you're happy to do bookstore readings – retailers appreciate reps who deliver for these events, so your reps will be glad to hear you're up for it.

The whirlwind months around publication can leave a novelist feeling like unplugging the phone and getting back to what they do best – writing, in solitude. But remember to maintain the relationships you've forged so far, with publicists and sales people in particular.

Troubleshooting

In this chapter you will learn:

▶ *How to respond positively and creatively to feedback from agents and publishers*

It's been fifteen years since I began working with first-time novelists who were struggling to find agents or publishers. I read their rejection letters carefully before I begin working on their novels – the feedback agents and publishers give is usually short, to the point and invaluable in finding a solution. Here are the most frequent reasons agents and publishers give for turning down a novel, with my advice on what to do if your agent or publisher requests a rethink.

I've been told that . . .

. . . my opening scenes are too slow.

Over-focus is usually the problem, when there are issues with pace in the opening pages. Naturally you've tried to zoom in on the world of your story and get under its skin, but sometimes a bold and surprising approach can work better than finely-represented detail. For example, if a thriller opens with someone getting on a train, walking past an unattended bag, then sitting down to read the sports page, we know what's going to happen. A canny thriller writer will get into this scene late, and open after the bomb's exploded. A first line like 'When I finally guessed the answer to 13-down in my morning crossword, I went to write it in and nothing happened; my pen was gone, as was my right arm' carries more impact and intrigue than a foregone conclusion.

. . . my opening scene needs thought. I don't agree; it's an action-packed, high-jeopardy streetfight for the hero, when he sees an old lady getting mugged. It's a believable everyday incident, and it shows how tough and principled the character is – why are agents telling me to rewrite it?

Opening sequences must establish character and situation whilst setting-up – or constituting – the first skirmish of your thriller's conflict. Unless the old lady or the muggers are directly connected to the plot, you're missing an opportunity to build pace and momentum in the story. The opening scenes should slingshot the action into the plot – if they're about unrelated incidents, and are included primarily to establish qualities in the protagonist, pace and intrigue suffers. Hook your readers into the plot from the very first scene, and slingshot the action forward as powerfully as you can.

. . . my opening chapters are weak, even though they cover a terrorist bombing. I think they've got topicality and tap into people's deepest fears, and I don't want to make the changes being suggested. Should I change agent instead?

Beware of 'topicality' or 'currency', or whatever you want to call it. The fact is that whatever's up-to-the-minute when a writer begins a novel is old news by the time they finish it. And don't think that because something is 'big' in the news that it's a big deal with people. Terrorist bombings, for example, have ravaged cities – in the UK and Europe, as well as less stable parts of the world – for the last half a century. They're something many people have grown up with, and grown a thick skin to. If you think that your plot will be a big hit with the public, but an agent or publisher tells you otherwise, then listen to them; they have more experience of bringing fiction to market than you do.

. . . my protagonist is wooden, even though I've written what's agreed to be an intriguing and interesting backstory for the character.

Writing 'backstory' is fun. The world is your oyster as you fill in the details of characters' time on the planet so far, devising circumstances and events to put flesh on the bones of characterization. But sometimes you can do too thorough a job – your character has experienced so much that there's no room left for growth. Remember that the key to developing lifelike characters is that their pasts should be as full of troubling loose ends and 'roads not taken' as the rest of us, only more so. Developing character is about planting seeds deep, and nurturing them carefully until it's time to make them flourish in the story.

. . . my villain isn't working on the page. The backstory is good, the circumstances of the story develop compellingly, but it's almost like everything's too perfectly villainous – when he speaks it's hard to stop him sounding like a cartoon villain. I've tried using the rule of 'Less is more' to strip it back to basics, but I'm told I need to rethink. Should I make this villain more human, more likable?

What a certain kind of villain needs is that rare combination of chilling menace and intriguing humanity. Think of Hannibal Lecter – he's a villain who can curdle our blood with barely a word, but at the same time we know he'd make for a much more interesting dinner-party guest than the protagonists of Thomas Harris' novels.

'Sympathy for the devil' is a twist writers have wrought for hundreds of years, all the way back to John Milton's *Paradise Lost* and Christopher Marlowe's *Doctor Faustus*, and it's one you can work too. It's all about exploiting that contrast between appearance and reality – circumstances may have compelled this person to shift their personal ethical boundaries, or dispense with them altogether, but were it not for that they'd be an interesting person to know.

. . . the pace lags across the story.

If you're hearing this, don't push for specifics. Instead, map out the key action of each scene in your draft in a flowchart – use a flipchart-sized piece of paper for this, or the back of an old poster. Use a red marker to map the core-value progressions through the story. Now look at the spaces in between the red. Pull these scenes from your typescript, lay them out in order, and draw a new flowchart for each one, then lay these charts in order. Are you choosing the absolute most efficient sequence of events between each core-value progression? If so, is there another way you can write these scenes – a new narrative perspective, a new pressure thrown into the mix, an event which can condense or leapfrog sequences within the progression? Now is the time to put your true creativity to work, as you open up options to add power and pace to your scene-designs, turning workhorse scene-sequences into taut, exciting progressions.

. . . my ending needs work.

Are you 'getting out early' enough from the plot? Or are you only hitting the end of the line at the very end of the story? Remember that satisfying stories need satisfying resolutions of their core-value progressions – resolutions which don't have to be positive, and can be entirely unexpected (think of Clarice Starling's progression in *The Silence of the Lambs*). Are you using all your opportunities to create surprise, in how you're handling your core values? The more you can spin your value progression, particularly toward its end, the greater the satisfaction for the reader.

Glossary of thriller genres

▶ **Action thriller**

Using plot to generate physical action and conflict, action thrillers typically choose a stripped-down narrative style so as not to impede the physical action. Conspiracies may be simple or complex in action thrillers, but need physical manifestation for a physical fightback. Action thrillers are often serials, using a 'series protagonist' for a succession of high-octane adventures. Action-thriller protagonists rarely arc, remaining essentially the same at the end of each adventure as they were at the start.

Unsurprisingly, this is the most venerable of the thriller genres. Its roots are in the 1930s and 1940s, in the work of American detective-fiction writers like Raymond Chandler and Dashiell Hammett, and of British action-adventure novelists like John Buchan and Geoffrey Household. The genre developed in conjunction with action cinema, with the suspense/chase movies of Alfred Hitchcock particularly influential. James Bond put the action-thriller at the heart of popular culture, with Robert Ludlum's creation Jason Bourne packing cinemas into the 21st century.

Key author: Lee Child

Key novel: *Without Fail*

▶ **Business thriller**

The action is primarily verbal combat and corporate power-play in a business thriller, so the genre is similar to *political* or *spy* thrillers – but when the world of the novel is a business corporation, it's unfettered by the obligations of an elected government or publicly funded secret-service. The business thriller has been successfully hybridized with *combat*, *political* and *spy* thrillers by many bestselling novelists. Michael Crichton wrote several fine business thrillers, in between the dinosaurs and sci-fi, refining the scope of the genre to focus on corporate sexual politics in *Disclosure*.

Key author: Michael Crichton

Key novel: *Rising Sun*

▶ Combat thriller

A military thriller, usually concerned with special operations. Often these novels are action-heavy versions of 'behind-enemy-lines' spy thrillers, using the same contrast between action on the ground and action back at HQ to generate friction. Combat adventure novels account for most publishing in this area, so true combat thrillers are rare.

Key author: Tom Clancy

Key novel: *Clear and Present Danger*

▶ Comic thriller

Standard thriller components are used to develop and resolve thriller style plots, but action sequences devolve into farce, played for laughs with often blackly comic outcomes – think of movies like *Men in Black* or *Tropic Thunder*. In fiction, the genre is often hybridized with another, e.g. fantasy in the case of Terry Pratchett.

Key author: Carl Hiaasen

Key novel: *Stormy Weather*

▶ Cop thriller

Often confused with the 'police procedural', which is the usual format for cops in mystery and crime fiction. James Patterson's Alex Cross is the most famous cop-thriller hero, but authors often deploy an 'off the leash' protagonist (excluded from duty for judicial reasons, between postings for career reasons, etc.) to free the action from the constraints of everyday rules and regulations.

Key author: Elmore Leonard

Key novel: *Out of Sight*

▶ Historical thriller

Typically concerned with great wars (e.g. the American Civil War, or the First World War) or similarly seminal periods in global statecraft. Often, effectively, a political or combat thriller which uses the opportunities and limitations of the historical period to generate original action. It's interesting to note that the most successful historical thrillers of recent decades work with an imaginary historical scenario (a Nazi victory in World War Two).

Key author: Robert Harris

Key novel: *Fatherland*

▶ Literary thriller

This is an often misused term. Literary thrillers aren't simply literary novels which feature a crime, or a couple of gunshots. A literary thriller uses an arcing protagonist in a basic thriller plot, but the conflict is generally psychological in nature, and the progress of the arcing protagonist is psychologically complex – therefore, a literary style is used to exploit nuance, and to carry the frequently negative outcome of literary-thriller plots.

Key author: Donna Tartt

Key novel: *The Secret History*

▶ Noir thriller

These use the components of *film noir* – an exhausted or disillusioned male protagonist, sometimes a *femme fatale* – to experiment with the three-act thriller form. They often challenge narrative conventions (e.g. a first-person 'voiceover' threaded through an otherwise third-person thriller, in Cormac McCarthy's *No Country For Old Men*), and are often set 'outside' society, as in McCarthy's border badlands, or inside Hollywood in Michael Tolkin's *The Player*. The experimentation of noir-thriller writers has been greatly influenced by post-modern ideas and perspectives, particularly since Hitchcock's seminal movie *North By North West* (1959).

Key author: James Sallis

Key novel: *And Death Will Have Your Eyes*

▶ Political thriller

Exposing what really goes down in the corridors of power, political thrillers thrive on devious double-dealing and behind-the-scenes manoeuvring. They differ from business-thrillers in that political appointees must pay lip-service to ethical principles. The fact that most secret-services are answerable to their political paymasters has enabled spy thrillers, particularly in the work of John le Carré, to draw deeply on the tension and intrigue of top-table political thrillers.

Key author: Frederick Forsyth

Key novel: *The Day of the Jackal*

▶ Sci-Fi thriller

An action or combat thriller set in the future. The antagonist typically embodies the futuristic element, whilst the hero tends to be a human very like ourselves.

Key author: Michael Crichton

Key novel: *Jurassic Park*

▶ Spy thriller

Also known as the 'espionage thriller', this genre evolved from Ian Fleming's action-adventure hybrids to the heavyweight entertainment of John le Carré's spy novels. These and the Jason Bourne movies exemplify the modern incarnation of the genre – novels about fighting and winning wars 'under the radar'. Le Carré often hybridizes his spy novels with political-thriller elements, reflecting the answerability of professional spies to the regimes which employ them.

Key author: John le Carré

Key novel: *Smiley's People*

▶ Supernatural thriller

Often confused with 'horror', particularly in the case of the genre's finest exponent Stephen King (for his first two decades of publishing, King's novels were almost all thrillers). In a supernatural thriller, the antagonist has qualities which are not found in nature – for example, a shark with a grudge in Peter Benchley's *Jaws* – or is itself a supernatural entity (e.g. the telekinesis which overwhelms Stephen King's abused teenager *Carrie*). Contemporary authors like Thailand-based John Burdett and Ireland's John Connolly have taken the genre into interesting new territory, creating successful hybridizations like the *supernatural cop thriller* (e.g. Burdett's *Bangkok Haunts*).

Key author: Stephen King

Key novel: *It*

Further reading and research

Thriller blogs are a great resource for new authors. They give the inside skinny on new novels and authors, and show a budding thriller writer the energy that's out there. Feel the pulse of the current crime and thriller scene at some of these excellent and energetic blogs, all of which carry plenty of links to other thriller-related sites:

▶ The Rap Sheet

Excellent thriller and crime blog with all the big stories from the scene, sharp writing and reviewing, and interesting in-depth articles about particular novels and authors. Also carries a long and comprehensive selection of links to other crime and thriller sites.

therapsheet.blogspot.co.uk

▶ Crime and publishing

Written by an agent, this is an excellent blog-style reviews site. Sound and often intriguing insights and perspectives from an industry insider.

crimeandpublishing.com

▶ Mysteries in paradise

Wide-ranging thriller, crime and mystery blog with reviews of new and re-issued classic novels. Each review has links to the best other reviews of each book, giving a quickly navigable overview of each new release. The site's own reviews are succinct and to the point, giving a valuable insight into what scores with a reader and what doesn't.

paradise-mysteries.blogspot.co.uk

▶ Scene of the crime

Interesting blog by a career thriller author, focusing on novels which use a strong sense of place.

jsydneyjones.wordpress.com

For more help with writing and selling your thriller, or if you'd like to explore the ideas of this book further visit Matthew Branton's website for new thriller authors:

http://www.thrillerauthor.info

Index